# Psychological
# Report Writing
## Assistant

# Psychological Report Writing Assistant

GARY GROTH-MARNAT

ARI DAVIS

WILEY

*Library of Congress Cataloging-in-Publication Data:*

Groth-Marnat, Gary.
    Psychological report writing assistant / Gary Groth-Marnat, Ari Davis.
      pages cm
    Includes bibliographical references and index.
    ISBN 978-0-470-88899-5 (paperback)
    ISBN 978-1-118-23485-3 (ebk.)
    ISBN 978-1-118-22110-5 (ebk.)
      1. Clinical psychology—Vocational guidance.   2. Medical assistants—Vocational guidance.
3. Neuropsychological report writing—Study and teaching.   4. Report writing—Study and teaching.   I. Davis, Ari.   II. Title.
  RC467.95.G76   2013
  616.89′023—dc23
                                                                            2013014059

Printed in the United States of America

SKY10038727_111822

*To Robin*

To Robin

# Contents

# Preface

Dear reader: Thank you for purchasing this book and its associated software. We hope that the material is clear and the guidelines, tools, strategies, and resources will make writing psychological reports easy, clear, integrated, focused, relevant—and fast. Most important, we hope it will allow readers to have a deeper understanding of the person being assessed and allow optimal decisions to be made.

Essential to the development of this book and software has been a set of core principles. One of these is the blending of the best of science combined with an appreciation for the art of doing clinical work. Both are interdependent. Science keeps art from becoming filled with bias and folklore. It allows us to be accountable for the conclusions and decisions we make. In contrast, art prevents science from becoming mechanistic and inhuman. It acknowledges the importance of wisdom, empathy, and using test results to understand the struggles and experience of the person. Thus, we hope that readers will find that built into the book and software is a deep appreciation and respect for both the art and science of assessment practice.

Successful efforts in academia seem to follow two possible strategies. One is to take simple information and make it as complex as possible. A second strategy is to take complex information and make it as simple and clear as possible. It is this second principle that we honor and hope we have infused into the book/software. For example, the second chapter of the book describes six core principles that create an optimal report. Each of these is accompanied by guidelines and strategies on how these can be implemented. Similarly, the software has been designed to organically follow the flow of writing a report and, at crucial points, to provide the report writer with guidelines, tools, examples, and resources. We hope that first-time users will easily understand the flow and tools, and that using the software will become even easier over the course of time.

A third principle has been to focus only on information that is most relevant for conducting the task of assessment and report writing. This has resulted in continual questioning of what is truly relevant. We have been cautioned that sometimes, when authors try to say too much, readers can become overwhelmed. The result is that many tools and strategies end up not getting used. Thus, we have focused only on including what we thought were essentials. Report writers themselves should similarly keep this in mind when they write reports. For example, including too many recommendations in a report can sometimes run the risk that none of them will be implemented because readers feel overwhelmed and don't know where to start.

A final principle has been writing for an unfilled niche. The sister book, *Handbook of Psychological Assessment*, now in its fifth edition, emerged from an unfilled need in the field. In the late 1970s and earlier, there was no comprehensive educational or professional book that covered the A–Z of how to conduct assessment. The *Handbook of Psychological Assessment* was designed to meet this need. Similarly, the current book and software were written to allow students/practitioners a source to walk them through the report writing process. This need became apparent during the process of many years of collaborating with students writing reports. It is and was a difficult skill to teach. Indeed, mastering the skills of writing a good, or any, report is often experienced as one of the hardest tasks in the training of professional psychologists. Experienced practitioners similarly struggle with writing reports, especially if they do so on an intermittent basis. Many practitioners who are experienced at report writing do things like collect common phrases or prepare lists of recommendations. They then use these phrases/recommendations to insert into reports at strategic places. These two strategies, as well as many others, were used in the development of the software. Given the clear challenges built into report writing, a book and expert system software seemed like something that would fill the need for a comprehensive tool that would facilitate the report writing process. We felt that not only should the process itself be facilitated, but tools and strategies offered should be based on what research has told us about what is involved in an optimal report. The findings and recommendations of this research have been integrated into both a philosophy of assessment and specific strategies of report writing.

Many people have generously given their time to advising, giving resources, and reviewing portions of this book and software. Professionals and researchers include the following: John Norcross provided his updated list and ratings of self-help books, films, and Internet resources; Larry Beutler consulted and reviewed material for Systematic Treatment Selection/InnerLife; Annie Chung submitted a sample psychoeducational report; Carol Kilgour submitted a sample personality report; Erik Lande provided his list of neuropsychological recommendations; Elisa Gothiel reviewed forensic material and made suggestions on recommendations; Richard Levak reviewed/discussed personality report organization; and both Rodney Lowman and David Donnay provided useful correspondence related to career/vocational reports. Particularly helpful have been my regular meetings with the following practicing psychologists in the Santa Barbara community: Erik Lande, Steve Smith, Jordan Witt, and Rebecca Goodman. They have all been helpful in allowing me to use them to clarify my ideas and compare them with their perspectives on applied assessment. In addition, the following students and professors have provided me with feedback on various portions of the book/software, including beta testing various modules of the software: Michael Mullard, George Ambrose, Aja Mutzel, and Wendy Eichler. In addition, Beta testers have included Anthony Bean, C. Holiday Blanchard, Paul Hamilton, Kristin Thompson, Kerri Bresette, Julia Michael, Jim Earnest, Caitlin Allen, and Card Kilgour.

There have also been a number of crucial publications in the field that provided both inspiration and resources. Although these were extremely useful, we also made careful efforts to alter these resources so that the information ended up being quite different from the original material. These include the following: Braaten's (2007) *The Child Clinician's Report Writing Handbook;* Jongsma and Peterson's (2006) *The Complete Adult Psychotherapy Planner* (4th ed.); Lichtenberger, Mather, Kaufman, and Kaufman's (2004) *Essentials of Assessment Report Writing;* Rusin and Jongsma's (2001) *The Rehabilitation Psychology Treatment Planner;* and Zuckerman's (2005) *Clinician's Thesaurus* (6th ed.).

# Introduction

The goal of psychological assessment is to integrate a variety of sources into a user-friendly, problem-focused, well-integrated psychological report that both describes a person and provides guidance in making optimal decisions. The above goal and associated procedures draw on a wide number of skills and knowledge ranging from technical psychometric knowledge to an ability to understand the lived experience of the persons being evaluated. Given these multiple demands, writing a high-quality psychological report is often a difficult task. This book and software will guide practitioners through the process of organizing and integrating data so as to provide accurate, user-friendly descriptions of persons being evaluated. These resources should not only improve the quality of reports, but should also make report writing more time efficient. It will also serve as a companion to and extension of Groth-Marnat's *Handbook of Psychological Assessment* (5th ed.).

## WHO THIS BOOK AND SOFTWARE ARE FOR

This book and software will be most useful for professional psychologists in training, beginning-level professional psychologists, and practicing professionals who write only occasional reports. It may also enable experienced assessment psychologists to write their reports more quickly and ensure that important dimensions of a report have not been overlooked. Specific resources included in this book are a description of the core qualities of optimal reports, report format, guidelines for completing various sections of the report, discussion of treatment recommendations, overview of different types of reports, and strategies for navigating the Psychological Report Writing Assistant (PRWA). Based on this

1

information, a wide number of corresponding resources have been incorporated into the PRWA software. The software is divided into modules for writing the following five most common types of reports: cognitive, neuropsychological, psychoeducational, personality, and forensic (see Chapter 3). It is hoped that report writers will use these resources to easily assemble assessment data into an integrated report. Ideally, writers will find the "voice" of an expert guiding them through each step of the process. The result should be that not only will report writing proceed more quickly, but the quality of reports will be significantly better than for persons not using the PRWA.

## Rationale and Philosophy for Report Writing: An Integrative Approach

The report writing rationale and philosophy incorporated in this book/software emphasizes integration and has been described by various authors (see Beutler & Groth-Marnat, 2003; Blais & Smith, 2008; Groth-Marnat, 2009a, 2009b; Harwood, Beutler, & Groth-Marnat, 2011; Kvaal, Choca, Groth-Marnat, Davis, 2011; Levak, Hogan, Beutler, & Song, 2011; Wright, 2011). Integration can be understood on several different levels. One essential feature of integration is making sense of apparent contradictions that often occur when reviewing assessment information. For example, a parent may report that his or her child has problems with attention, but, when formally assessed, the child's test scores appear in the average/normal range. A possible reason for this discrepancy may be that the test situation is highly structured such that the child followed the directions of the assessor and did not have to compete with real-world distractions. His or her performance outside the assessment situation might be quite different. Another example might be scores on a self-report instrument such as the Personality Assessment Inventory that indicate that the client has an absence of disordered thoughts. In contrast, the Rorschach might indicate quite confused thinking, possibly consistent with an underlying thought disorder. This may be due to the more ambiguous, less structured, performance-based task of the Rorschach's being more sensitive to the presence of a subtle, underlying thought disorder. An integrative approach would work to make sense of these contradictions, and only when these contradictions were resolved would a narrative interpretation be developed and inserted into the report. In contrast, many traditional approaches to writing a report simply discuss test results one test at a time (e.g., "Test scores on the Personality Assessment Inventory indicate . . . ," etc.). The most problematic example of this would be simply cutting and pasting from an interpretive text or a computer-generated computer narrative "interpretation." One purpose of this book is to expand on contradictory assessment results along with suggestions on how to resolve them. In addition, the Psychological Report Writing Assistant provides an Integrated Information Manager that helps users integrate their assessment results into integrated interpretations focusing on various domains of functioning.

Another central feature of this book and software is integrating the results of assessment with the consumer. The consumer refers to both the referral source as well as the person being evaluated. Integration with the referral source first of all means understanding their needs and expectations. This typically begins with carefully clarifying the referral questions. This can often be done by exploring what client decisions need to be made. It also means understanding the context the referral source is working in (see Chapter 5). For example, reports written within a medical context would mean that the report writer should become knowledgeable regarding options for cognitive and other forms of rehabilitation. This should be reflected in the type of assessment information that is obtained as well as the choice of recommendations. Another example is that sometimes referrals from school settings don't want recommendations included in reports because it is often felt that recommendations should be developed by a team rather than by the individual psychologist. These and many other considerations are discussed and will enable report writers to best integrate their reports into various assessment settings.

Another example of integrating the report with referral sources is to make sure that the interpretations made about the client are accurate. While this may seem obvious, reports that focus solely on tests and test scores can potentially provide considerable inaccurate information by providing cut-and-paste "interpretations" and qualify these by saying "People with these types of profiles . . . ." The inaccuracy of unintegrated cut-and-paste interpretations is highlighted in that typically half of all interpretations generated by computer-based reports will not be accurate for the person being assessed (see the section on core strategy 3 in Chapter 2). However, the referral source may mistakenly believe that all or most of the descriptors listed will be accurate. Thus, it is incumbent on clinicians to work with interpretive descriptors to determine which ones are, and which ones are not, accurate for their client. The Psychological Report Writing Assistant's Integrated Information Manager will help clinicians to organize their information and thus more easily make these differentiations. It should also be emphasized that for some reports, particularly in forensic settings, it may be desirable and even necessary to stay close to the "facts" by describing test scores and then detailing the reasoning process the clinician used in coming to their opinions. In these cases, the integration of results is typically placed in the summary rather than the impressions and interpretations (and summary).

Integration also involves using language that connects with and makes sense to both the referral source and the client. Thus, an integrative report is typically written in user-friendly, everyday language that is clear while still being sufficiently professional. There is minimal use of jargon, tests scores, statistics, and the clinician's reasoning processes. For example, instead of simply stating the defense mechanism of "rationalization," report writers are encouraged to write something like ". . . the client convinces himself that no wrongs were done by developing convenient excuses that make himself look acceptable to himself and others." The PRWA uses a search function to identify common examples of overly technical and other forms of problematic language. Once these are highlighted, a rationale is given for why the phrases might be problematic, and alternative language is provided that can be easily extracted, edited, and integrated into the report. User-friendly language is also encouraged in the form of giving everyday examples of the types of problems the client might confront. For example, a client with poor spatial skills might have problems following maps, understanding directions, or finding where something is in a house. In addition, user-friendly language is encouraged in reports through using wording that indicates empathy, is likely to facilitate change, and tries to understand the world through the perspective of the client (see Finn, 2012; Finn, Fischer, & Handler, 2012; Fischer, 2012; Levak, Siegel, Nichols, & Stolberg, 2011). For example, instead of stating that a histrionic-type client is "somatizing," "dissociating," and "converting," report writers might alternatively describe the person as follows: ". . . She is working so hard to hold her feelings inside and trying to stay positive that these efforts are putting stress on her body, and this is most likely why she is experiencing headaches, backaches, and neck aches." (Levak et al., 1991)

A further goal of integration is that components of the report connect, flow, summarize, answer the referral question, and are easily accessible. In particular, it should be clear what the report is intending to do, and it should be easy to determine whether it has accomplished these goals. One strategy is to connect the referral questions with corresponding and numbered answers to these questions. The PRWA software provides various formats and guidelines to help ensure that the report is structured in a clear, coherent manner such that the various components of the report are most likely to accomplish its intended goals. In addition, the language should be easy to read. This can be enhanced by using a wizard embedded into the PRWA that easily provides users with a menu of common report writing phrases. In some cases these are entire paragraphs for interpretive domains that can be edited based on information derived from the client and organized using the Integrated Information Manager.

A final principle is that recommendations need to be integrated with the needs of the referral source, client, and resources in the community. They should also be sufficiently comprehensive. The PRWA provides suggestions, guidelines, and examples that should enhance this process. In addition, there is a wizard in the form of a comprehensive menu of recommendations tailored toward each type of psychological report. Users of the program can easily transfer these recommendations into their reports, where they can be further edited to address the specifics of the case. The menu of recommendations is sufficiently broad that it will help users to consider a full range of possibilities organized according to treatment, referral, placement, further evaluation, alteration in environment, and self-help.

The preceding principles represent an ideal. Various sources have recommended many of these principles (see Armengol, Kaplan, & Moes, 2001; Beutler & Groth-Marnat, 2003; Blais & Smith, 2008; Brenner, 2003; Groth-Marnat, 2009a, 2009b; Harvey, 2006; Levak & Hogan, 2011). Despite these recommendations, the modal report in practice is often suboptimal (Groth-Marnat & Horvath, 2006; Harvey, 2006; Tallent, 1993). This research, often based on consumer feedback, makes it clear that report writers often become focused on individual test scores, write reports that are difficult to understand, and often do not work to resolve contradictory assessment results (Harvey, 2006; Levak & Hogan, 2011). The results are reports that are not well received by consumers, are filled with jargon, are overly technical, describe test scores rather than clients, and do not connect to the client's everyday life experience (Groth-Marnat, 2009a; Groth-Marnat & Horvath 2006; Harvey, 2006). Once this pattern is established in graduate training, clinicians are likely to continue to write suboptimal reports throughout the remainder of their career.

The reasons for poorly written reports are numerous. Harvey (1997, 2006) found that professionals in training were likely to write overly technical, non–user-friendly reports for the following reasons: they were taught to provide data without explaining the data sufficiently; they had limited awareness that many readers will not understand the terms that are used; and they lacked clarity regarding the intended audience. In addition, reports that focused on tests and test scores were easier and quicker to write since they required less conceptual effort on the part of the writer. In other words, the tests dictate what will be written rather than the integration of more complex and sometimes contradictory information. In addition, the sheer number of report writing guidelines presented to practitioners often means it is easy to overlook some of these guidelines.

## An Introduction to the Psychological Report Writing Assistant

The PRWA has been prepared to assist professional psychologists in writing high-quality reports. Knowing how to develop high-quality reports is based in part on knowing the core strategies involved in preparing the types of reports that are likely to be well received by consumers. These core strategies are not only detailed in Chapter 2, but are integrated throughout the PRWA software. The PRWA itself is a highly graphic, interactive program that has been developed as a software tutor and expert system. The orientation of the PRWA is to combine education with professional assistance in an entertaining and intuitive medium. The PRWA guides the report writer through the principal phases of report development that are most conducive to comprehensiveness, integrated interpretation, therapeutic insight, and optimum recommendations in clear response to the referral questions. The application toolkit provides clinical reasoning Wizards and a knowledge base for work in the educational, psychiatric, legal, psychological clinic, and medical consultation venues.

When working through the PRWA, practitioners fill in the required data based on the appropriate template for a cognitive, neuropsychological, personality, psychoeducational, or forensic report. Throughout report development, the PRWA displays a hierarchical outline of the report that maintains a view of the whole while defining the proper sequence, structure, and necessary categories of information most relevant for the referral source and referral questions. While working on a defined section of the report, the user is supervised with context- and topic-sensitive professional guidelines, exemplary sample text, and client information that have been previously integrated across domains and test instruments for the section of the report under development. By clicking on various sections of the report outline, users can easily and quickly bring the desired section of the report into view for editing.

The feature set and multiphased working environment of the PRWA allows the preceding toolset to accommodate a wide variety of requirements and specifications. It helps users to answer the referral questions in a professionally succinct, communicable manner, which narrates the personal story of the individual and promotes the optimum treatment recommendations for collaborative discussion and implementation.

The PRWA includes numerous useful phrases, alerts report writers to potentially problematic phrases, and provides a comprehensive menu of recommendations tailored to different types of reports. Sample phrases are included throughout the software. Examples include how to articulate interpretations and to express appropriate opinions (e.g.,"The findings are consistent with although not necessarily diagnostic of . . ."). In addition, there is a scan function that can review the draft of the report and identify areas that might be problematic. Such areas might include overly technical language, inaccurate terminology, too much detailing of reasoning processes, colloquialisms, or language suggesting that the assessment results have not been adequately integrated. The alerts provide a rationale as to why the phrases might be problematic as well as suggestions on how the section could be reworded. A final feature is extensive lists of recommendations tailored to the various types of reports. These can be added to the draft of the report by simply putting a check next to the recommendation. Guidelines are provided on how the recommendations can be edited to best meet the requirements of the report.

RAPID REFERENCE 1.1: KEY FEATURES OF THE PSYCHOLOGICAL REPORT WRITING ASSISTANT

- Modules for five categories of reports: cognitive, neuropsychological, personality, psychoeducational, and forensic
- Guidelines for constructing subsections of reports
- Composition screen with wizards linking resources to facilitate report writing
- Sample reports with sections linked to guidelines
- Integrated Information Manager
- Menu of common phrases that can be inserted into report narrative and edited
- Search wizard to identify problem ("red flag") phrases: listing of phrase, rationale for why it might be problematic, suggestions for alternative wording
- Menu of recommendations
- Wizard for developing psychotherapy treatment recommendations

The preceding information provides a general overview of the PRWA. Additional features are described throughout the book. In addition, Chapter 6 details the major features and provides specific operating instructions. Each of the instructions is illustrated with relevant screenshots.

## FROM SOFTWARE TO THE REAL WORLD

In order to develop the PRWA, it was necessary to decide on common formats and to emphasize an integrated, user-friendly style of presentation. This was based on the implications of research on psychological reports combined with over 30 years of teaching assessment, clinical experience, and reviewing thousands of reports. At the same time, it should be emphasized that there is no single way to write a report. Sometimes report writers may wish to edit various sections of reports based on their own preferences. Often, agencies have their own format with corresponding guidelines that all employees are required to follow. There may also be other idiosyncratic aspects of the assessment context or demands of the referral source that strongly influence how a report is written. For example, the resources provided in this book and the PRWA emphasize not using jargon and minimizing references to tests and test scores. However, there may be situations where it may be necessary to use technical terms as well as to detail test results. It should be noted, however, that there is flexibility built into the PRWA to enable report writers to edit all aspects of their reports according to their needs. Report writers should always consider the guidelines, strategies, examples, and recommendations provided in this book/software program, but the decision is ultimately based on the report writer's unique situation and background.

The report formats presented in this book and the PRWA were developed to be generic and sufficiently broad so that most components of reports would be included. It should be acknowledged that other guides to writing reports have sometimes used different titles for the various subsections. For example, the Background Information section has sometimes been referred to as "Relevant History," and the "Impressions and Interpretations" section has sometimes been referred to as the "Discussion" or "Findings." In addition, some report guidelines have sections/subsections such as "History of the Problem," "Substance Abuse History," or "Legal History." In the PRWA this information is subsumed under different subsections. However, it should be easy for users to insert and reorganize their reports by adding new sections or subsections if they choose to do so.

Another and similar issue is that the subsections included in the "Impressions and Interpretations" section have been purposely developed to be overinclusive. In other words, there are a number of subsections/domains that users would be unlikely to actually use for a specific report on a client. The reason for this is to provide report writers with guidelines and examples for as many options as possible. One example of overinclusiveness found in the domains for personality report templates in the PRWA includes subsections for verbal abilities, processing speed, and memory; however, including these domains is usually not appropriate for a personality report. Another example occurs in cognitive/neuropsychological reports, where the PRWA has included domains for personality, interpersonal, and coping style, and yet these domains may also not be necessary to include. In each of these examples, domains were developed and were creatively expanded to include examples of how these subsections might be written should they be needed. It was sometimes difficult to balance being too specific for a certain type of report with being overly general and inclusive. Hopefully, users will be understanding of this dilemma and exercise flexibility in choosing which of the subsections they would like to include.

The items in the menus for common phrases and recommendations were selected based on what seemed would be the most useful for report writers. These phrases were derived from reading numerous reports and collections of phrases and recommendations derived from clinical practice. Phrases were also developed to be consistent with the strategies and philosophy of the book. Thus, interpretive paragraphs were developed that can be edited but that also exemplify the use of everyday language, qualitative observations, and everyday examples. Valuable resources used in developing the common phrases and recommendations were Braaten's *The Child Clinician's Report Writing Handbook* (2007), Jongsma and Peterson's *The Complete Adult Psychotherapy Planner* (4th ed., 2006), Rusin and Jongsma's *The Rehabilitation Psychology Treatment Planner* (2001), and Zuckerman's *Clinician's Thesaurus* (6th ed., 2005). If report writers would like more comprehensive phrases and recommendations, they are encouraged to consult these sources. What emerged for the PRWA were lists of common phrases and recommendations that seemed frequently used, clear, and not overwhelmingly comprehensive.

Users of PRWA should be able to quickly screen the menus and select which, if any, phrases and recommendations might be appropriate for their report. Only the phrases/recommendations that seemed fairly commonly used were included in order to keep the number of options at a manageable level. Many of the common phrases/recommendations are similar across each of the report modules. However, there are also phrases/recommendations that are specific to each of the modules. For example, cognitive/neuropsychological modules emphasize areas such as cognitive rehabilitation, whereas the forensic module focuses more on forensic-specific recommendations such as category of incarceration or options for child custody.

As noted, the philosophy of integrative report writing emphasizes an individualized, humanistic, empathic approach that works to resolve contradictions and connect with the life, experience, and context of the client. Various strategies in the PRWA have been developed to enhance this orientation. Using these can also make report writing quite time efficient. There is some danger in overutilizing these editable phrases and paragraphs in that report writing could devolve into a mechanistic, cookie-cutter, cut-and-paste approach in which one size fits all. This may occur if a time-pressed clinician simply inserts an editable paragraph into a report without carefully considering if all the components described in the paragraph are both accurate and relevant for their client. This same clinician may also quickly edit the paragraph and move on to a new section of the report without also considering whether there is further information that should be added. This approach is, of course, strongly discouraged, and report writers should be continually vigilant that this doesn't occur. Hopefully, other strategies built into the PRWA (e.g., Integrated Information Manager, red flag phrases, subsection guidelines) will guard against this potential problem.

A further consideration is that there is a search function to identify red flag phrases. These are followed by a rationale as to why the identified word, phrase, or sentence might be problematic, as well as examples of how the phrase might be rewritten. The red flag phrases include things such as technical language (jargon), strong reference to test scores, phrases suggesting minimal integration of results, and detailing the clinicians' reasoning processes. It should be emphasized that rewriting the various red flag phrases should always be done at the discretion of the clinician writing the report. There will certainly be instances in which using technical language, adhering to test scores, not fully integrating assessment results, and detailing the clinician's reasoning processes might be warranted. Examples might be that report writers need to adhere to an organization's policy to liberally insert test scores; medical settings might expect clinicians to use technical medical language; or forensic examiners may need to detail their reasoning processes. However, it is hoped that, at the very least, report writers will seriously consider the rationale for why the red flag phrases might be problematic and then decide whether this perspective is relevant for their report.

One struggle in writing this book and associated software was which categories of reports to use as examples. Much of this struggle stemmed from the sometimes ambiguous differentiation of one type of report from another. For example, a neuropsychological report might also be used for forensic purposes. As a result, it might become more a forensic report than a purely neuropsychological report. From a practical perspective, this means that clinicians would need to be knowledgeable regarding the guidelines and strategies for both types of reports. One distinction that is important to clarify is between cognitive and neuropsychological reports. Cognitive assessment seems somewhat broader than neuropsychological assessment in that cognitive assessment might originate from questions regarding clients having a thought disorder, needing career guidance, or wanting academic placement. General cognitive assessments are also likely to be needed in general psychology/counseling clinics and conducted as part of the expected knowledge base of professional psychologists. As a result, professionals in training are typically first taught how to develop cognitive assessment for these contexts. In contrast, neuropsychological assessments are more likely to focus on neurologically related disorders, occur in medical settings, and be conducted by specialty neuropsychologists. As a result of the distinction between cognitive and neuropsychological reports, the PRWA has included these as two separate modules.

It is hoped that readers and users of the PRWA will understand, apply, and deepen their appreciation for what should be its clear assets and resources. At the same time, there should be an appreciation, tolerance, and correction for the various limitations of the PRWA. It cannot do everything, cover all situations, and especially cannot be expected to cover all types of reports. However, there are principles built into the PRWA that will guide the reader toward integration, client uniqueness, and empathy. At the same time, there are software tools that may result in users' overutilizing cut-and-paste material that could result in actually obscuring client and context uniqueness. In addition, sometimes the distinction between types of reports is not as clear as was desired. While most of the PRWA strategies and resources provide external tools for the report writer, there is also no substitute for critical thinking, clinical judgment, knowledge of the referral setting, wisdom, empathy, and understanding the client's experience of his or her world. It is hoped that the strengths of the PRWA will be utilized as much as possible, its limitations will be compensated for, and clinicians will continue to develop their professional competencies. The result should be high-quality reports that enhance understanding, answer questions, improve decision making, and reduce suffering.

## AN OVERVIEW OF HOW TO USE THIS BOOK AND SOFTWARE

The book portion of the PRWA takes the reader through the philosophy, essential information, and guidelines on how to write optimal psychological reports. The information should follow a logical sequence that begins in the first chapter with the rationale for how the principles of report writing were developed and what constitutes an integrated report. Key features of the approach described in the PRWA are that report writers should integrate the components of the report in order to answer the referral question; contradictions appearing in assessment information are resolved; interpretations are organized according to domains and are expanded to connect with the client's world; everyday language is used that connects with a wide audience; and recommendations are provided that are comprehensive and connect with the needs of both the client and the referral source.

As previously noted, this chapter provides an introduction to report writing combined with an introduction to PRWA. Chapter 2 describes the core qualities of a good report. Chapter 3 provides the structure and guidelines for writing a psychological report. This summarizes essential material along with concrete strategies on how to write an optimal report. Chapter 4 elaborates on various strategies and types of recommendations. Chapter 5 describes the most frequent types of reports. This will enable readers to understand the major similarities and differences among these reports. Included will be key considerations such as what types of information referral sources in different contexts are looking for, domains that are most often included, and tips on how to word the reports. These qualities are a theme that runs through both the book and software portions of PRWA.

Chapter 6 provides readers with a manual for using the software features of the PRWA. This begins with an initial description of the first screenshot. The opening screenshot is important to understand since it provides instruction and images of how the rest of the software flows through the report writing process. It also provides icons related to the wizards and other resources embedded in the program. Other sections of Chapter 6 illustrate how to use various software features, including entering client information, the report template, report guidelines, composition screen, examples of how to write sections of the reports, types of reports, common phrase wizard, red flag wizard, recommendation wizard, and using Systematic Treatment Selection. Even though Chapter 6 provides a road map for using the PRWA, it is still hoped that the software will be sufficiently intuitive for users to readily write a report without needing to search for clarification. However, when report writers need to gain more detail on various aspects of the PRWA, they can consult Chapter 6. Chapter 6 has also been conveniently expanded and inserted into the PRWA software and can be accessed by clicking onto the User Manual or Help icon.

# Recommended Reading

Brenner, E. (2003). Consumer-focused psychological assessment. *Professional Psychology: Research and Practice, 34*, 240–247.

Groth-Marnat, G., & Horvath, L. S. (2006). The psychological report: A review of current controversies. *Journal of Clinical Psychology, 62*, 73–81.

Levak, R. W., & Hogan, S. (2011). Integrating and applying assessment information: Decision making, patient feedback, and consultation. In T. M. Harwood, L. E. Beutler, & G. Groth-Marnat (Eds.), *Integrative assessment of adult personality* (3rd ed., pp. 373–412). New York, NY: Guilford Press.

Lichtenberger, E. O. (2006). Computer utilization and clinical judgment in psychological assessment reports. *Journal of Clinical Psychology, 62*, 19–32. doi: 10.1002/jclp.20197

# CHAPTER 2

# Core Qualities of a Good Report: Principles and Strategies

The previous chapter presented material on the philosophy of integrative assessment and general principles of report writing. In order to guide practitioners, six core strategies of a high-quality report have been developed. These six strategies involve concrete, specific guidelines, and can be achieved by using resources included within this book and embedded within the Psychological Report Writing Assistant (PRWA). The core qualities have been derived by following the recommendations of research done on reports combined with evaluating several thousand reports written by both experienced professional psychologists and graduate students. These strategies involve clearly connecting the referral questions with the answers to the corresponding answer to these questions, enhancing report readability, organizing interpretations according to functional domains, minimizing test-oriented language, integrating interpretations, and developing broad, relevant recommendations (see Rapid Reference 2.1). These strategies are briefly described in this chapter, and many of the themes are covered in more depth in subsequent chapters.

## 1. ANCHORING REFERRAL QUESTIONS TO THE SUMMARY/RECOMMENDATIONS

Most reports list the referral questions in the referral question section and, to a greater or lesser extent, answer the questions in the summary/recommendations. It is recommended that the question to summary link should be strengthened as much as possible. This can be done by using several clear, easily implemented techniques. However, a prereq-uisite to adequately answering the referral questions is that the questions themselves must be clear and can actually be answered by psychologi-cal assessment (see the Referral Question section in Chapter 3). Once the questions have been refined, they can be listed in the referral section by numbering each of the questions. The Summary/Recommendations section should include a corresponding subsection in which the referral questions are listed in an abbreviated form and succinctly answered. The same numbers used to list the referral questions in the Referral Question section should be used to number the answers to these questions in the Summary/Recommendations section.

The preceding strategy should result in clear, focused, strong links between the beginning of the report and the end. It is also consistent with the overarching purpose of a psychological assessment to provide clear, strong answers to the referral questions. It removes any doubt on the part of the reader that the clinician has done his or her best to address the purpose of the assessment. If done properly, the reader should be able to know the essential findings of the report by reading the list-ing of referral questions at the beginning of the report and then reading the answers to each of these questions in the relevant Summary subsec-tion. Following is an example of a list of numbered referral questions followed by the answers to these questions. It should be noted, however, that because the example below was written for a forensic evaluation, the

---

**RAPID REFERENCE 2.1: THE SIX CORE STRATEGIES FOR A GOOD REPORT**

1. Clearly connect the referral questions to answers to these questions in the summary/recommendations sections.
2. Make the report readable.
3. Organize interpretations according to functional domains.
4. Minimize test-oriented language and test scores.
5. Integrate interpretations with all sources of data and connect to the cli-ent's world.
6. Make recommendations broad, integrated with interpretations, and connected to the client's world.

answers to the referral questions are most appropriately labeled as "opinions" rather than "answers."

My understanding is that Mr. Jones is facing legal decisions specific to transferring his home in Metroville from a revocable trust to an irrevocable trust. As a result, you need to better understand the following questions:

1. To what extent can he comprehend the legal information that he is confronting?
2. To what extent can he appreciate the significance of this information?
3. Can he express a choice (donative intent)?
4. Does he have the cognitive capacity to transfer durable power of attorney?
5. To what extent might he be susceptible to undue influence?

These questions are listed below and were answered in the Summary and Recommendations section.

Given the information detailed in the above report, my opinions to your referral questions are summarized below:

1. *Comprehension of legal information.* Mr. Jones can comprehend the basic components of changing his house from a revocable to an irrevocable trust.
2. *Appreciate the significance of this information.* Although Mr. Jones can appreciate the basic meaning of changing his house from a revocable to an irrevocable trust, I have concerns that he may not recall previous relevant information due to the severity of his memory impairment. He has little capacity to consolidate recent facts or events and, without such information, would have a difficult time fully evaluating new events or decisions. Accordingly, appropriate supervision and consultation should be available to him.
3. *Express a choice (donative intent).* Mr. Jones is capable of expressing a choice and has done so quite clearly. He is aware that he has the asset (his home), would like to place it into an irrevocable trust, and is aware that such a decision cannot be changed once it has been made legally binding.
4. *Have the capacity to transfer durable power of attorney.* Mr. Jones does have the capacity to express a preference for someone to be his durable

power of attorney. He would be able to understand the meaning of the term and the implications this would have for him.

5. *Subject to undue influence.* Given his memory impairment, he would potentially be vulnerable to undue influence. He would have considerable difficulty recalling recent events to assist him in resisting influence from others. He is aware of his memory deficits and, due to this awareness, does not trust his own ability. As a result, he would be susceptible to being unduly influenced by the memory and reasoning of a person he trusted.

## 2. Making the Report Readable

All reports should, of course, be written clearly. While this may seem obvious, research has indicated that reports are usually rated by consumers as being too technical, filled with jargon, overly wordy, and written at a reading level far above the typical readers of reports (Brenner, 2003; Harvey, 2006; Pelco, Ward, Coleman, & Young, 2009). For example, Harvey (1997) noted that most reports were written at a 15- to 16-year level of education. In contrast, 72% of parents who were likely to read reports about their children were found to have a below-12-year educational level. She concluded that reports are generally written near the educational level of the psychologists writing the reports. In a later study, Harvey (2006) stated that professional psychologists in training often write reports to impress their supervisor and bolster their prestige rather than to clearly communicate with the referral source. The style of report writing evolving from these motivations often extends into later professional practice. The wider conclusion is that most reports seem to be written more for other psychologists than for a broader audience. Shectman (1979) also concluded this when he said, "All too often, I fear, we write for our supervisors or each other under the guise of writing for a colleague" (p. 784). In contrast, the ethical code for psychologists states that assessment results are supposed to be presented in a clear, understandable manner.

The main things that can be done to create greater clarity are to use short sentences, minimize the number of difficult words, reduce acronyms, and increase the use of subheadings (Harvey, 1997, 2006). In addition to using short, concise sentences, paragraphs should be well constructed. The first sentence of a paragraph should both introduce the topic of the paragraph and provide a global statement. The remainder of the paragraph should expand the first sentence by including more specific information. For example, a paragraph might begin with a general statement about a client's executive functioning ("Ms. Jones's executive abilities were mildly impaired"). This might be followed by more specific information related to smaller details of what is meant by executive functioning (". . . difficulty initiating behavior, problems flexibly changing her responses, poor awareness of her difficulties . . .") and behavioral observations (". . . the client needed to frequently be reminded to begin her responses and, when working on tasks, would repeatedly make the same response . . .").

---

### RAPID REFERENCE 2.2: MAKE THE REPORT READABLE

- Use short sentences.
- Minimize difficult words.
- Minimize acronyms.
- Organize paragraphs: general statement followed by specifics.
- Use subheadings.

---

Report writers should also minimize the number of difficult words, including the reduction or elimination of jargon and acronyms. Some report writers might argue for the use of jargon by pointing out that it provides a professional polish to a report, adds to the prestige of the report, is a clear means of communicating with colleagues, and is a shorthand means of communicating. This is countered by findings that seemingly clear technical terms are frequently misunderstood even by trained professionals (Brenner, 2003; Harvey, 1997; Pelco et al., 2009). In addition, using technical terms means the report will be understood by a more restricted audience and serves to reduce the readability of the report.

The preceding recommended strategies should enhance the readability of reports not only for professional psychologists but also for a wider audience. The PRWA has alerts built into the program to identify common jargon, describe the rationale for not using the jargon, and give suggested recommendations. For example, a report writer might use the term *auditory immediate memory*. The PRWA would then allow report writers to conduct a search that would highlight the term *auditory immediate memory* with information that would say: "This is an example of jargon and may not be easily understood by readers of your report. SUGGESTION: Translate into more everyday language by writing something like '. . . short-term memory for information he has heard. . . .'"

The preceding techniques for increasing readability would ideally result in a report writing style that is clear and uses everyday language but is still professional but not complex. Following are some examples of translating highly complex information into more readable, less complex statements. The first example is derived from a standard set of MMPI-2 descriptors for an elevation on scale 1/Hypochondriasis (see Groth-Marnat, 2009a, pp. 237–238). This is contrasted with client feedback statements describing similar client dynamics and adapted from Levak et al. (1990). The feedback statements are not only more readable, but they are also phrased in such a way as to be more empathic and facilitate client growth.

> *High complexity description from MMPI-2 Scale 1/Hypochondriasis:* "While they have a reduced level of efficiency, they are rarely completely incapacitated. They will use their symptom-related complaints to manipulate others thereby creating interpersonal distress."
>
> *Low complexity description from MMPI-2 Scale 1/Hypochondriasis:* "Their body is a constant source of anxiety and fear for them. So much of their time is spent worrying about their physical well-being, it is hard for them to accomplish anything, and to find outside interests or things they can do that will not incur additional pain. They may have developed a number of ways to get people to help them. At the same time, however, they resent not being able to do things for themselves."

The following additional example is provided by Harvey (1997) and includes a high- versus a low-complexity progress statement.

> *High complexity description* (reading grade level of 16): "The daily group therapy meetings improved Albert's communication skills and gave him

a place for receiving adult and peer support in an interpersonal context. He often took a provocative stance, and sometimes challenged staff leadership in group meetings. He continues to need help resisting his proclivity for using his tried and true coercive behavior as a way of getting what he wants."

*Low complexity description* (reading grade level of 9): "Daily group therapy was held to improve Albert's ability to talk with others, both adults and students his age. Sometimes Albert tried to take the leadership of the group away from the adults. He often tried to provoke them. Other students Albert's age tried to help him learn to take turns and share with others. Staff also praised Albert when he made a positive contribution or was cooperative. He still needs help avoiding his habit of using misbehavior to get his way." (pp. 273–274)

The final example translates jargon in the form of a common defense mechanism and translates it into a readable definition using everyday language.

"The client uses *reaction formation* . . ." can be translated into ". . . the client takes wishes or feelings that create anxiety and turns them into the opposite of what she wants or feels."

A final clear, easily achievable recommendation to enhance clarity is to use subheadings. This is most relevant for the Background Information and the Impressions and Interpretations sections. These allow the reader to easily find relevant portions of the report (see Chapter 3).

## 3. IMPRESSIONS AND INTERPRETATIONS ORGANIZED ACCORDING TO DOMAINS

A strong recommendation for report writing is to present the interpretations according to functional domains (e.g., coping style, memory, interests). The domains to include will be determined by a combination of the type of report (see Chapter 5) and the referral question. For example, a neuropsychological evaluation will typically organize the functional domains according to attention, language, spatial abilities, memory, and executive functions. In contrast, a psychoeducational assessment might include domains for general intellectual abilities, verbal abilities, and achievement, including reading, spelling, and math. Additional domains might be included based on the needs of the assessment. For example, a career assessment might also include an additional domain for managerial style, or the neuropsychological report might need to also include a domain for sensorimotor functioning. Most professional psychologists begin writing a report based on their own preferred template for domains and then vary these according to the needs of the assessment.

Presenting interpretations according to functional domains is preferred because it is comprehensive and provides a good sense of the person. However, it also requires professional psychologists to integrate the results. In other words, interpretations, even within the domains, should not be merely giving the results of one test. Instead, all sources of relevant information should be used to make the interpretations included within the domain. For example, if a client has excellent verbal abilities, this conclusion should not only be based on something like the Wechsler Adult Intelligence Scale–IV (WAIS-IV) Verbal Comprehension Index, but also be supported by behavioral observations of the client during the assessment session along with relevant history. A potential problem with this format for presenting interpretations is that it is initially likely to be more time consuming than presenting interpretations test by test. The PRWA assists in this process by using the Integrated Information Manager that allows users to complete a grid that summarizes relevant domains with categories of assessment information. The grid can be customized given the domains of interest (e.g., verbal abilities, coping style) combined with the various types of assessment information (e.g., WAIS-IV, behavioral observations). Notes can be made in each of the boxes that intersect the domains of interest with the types of assessment information (see Figure 2.1). Once the notes have been entered, the essential interpretations can be extracted and written as integrated paragraphs according to functional domains.

In contrast to the preceding suggestion to present interpretations according to functional domains is to present interpretations test-by-test (i.e., WAIS-IV, Personality Assessment Inventory [PAI], etc.). This style usually begins various sections by stating something like "Results of the MMPI-2 indicate . . ." or "On the Psychological Assessment Inventory, the client. . . ." The primary advantage of this style is that it allows the reader to determine where the interpretations came from. A further advantage of this style is that it is relatively easy to report the results.

| FIGURE 2.1 | INTEGRATED INFORMATION MANAGEMENT GRID (ABBREVIATED) |
| --- | --- |

| Topics | Interview | WAIS-IV | WMS-IV | Trail Making | COWAT |
| --- | --- | --- | --- | --- | --- |
| General level of intellectual function | | | | | |
| Verbal skills | | | | | |
| Perceptual organization (nonverbal abilities) | | | | | |

This is particularly the case if report writers simply list the interpretations included under elevated scores for something like an MMPI-2 code type or a high score on a WAIS-IV index.

Despite the advantages of test-by-test reporting of interpretations, there are also some very clear disadvantages. The main one is that test-by-test reporting is likely to produce interpretations that are not accurate. This is most likely to occur when clinicians simply list the interpretations given in an interpretive guide or computer-generated "report." It should be emphasized that authors of these interpretive guides are not really presenting them as "interpretations" but more as "interpretive hypotheses." In other words, they may or may not be true for the person. In many cases, only about half of the "interpretations" will accurately describe the person (Butcher, Perry, & Atlis, 2000). Since professional psychologists are required to ensure the accuracy of the information they provide, a cut-and-paste strategy is likely to be considered unethical (McMinn, Buchanan, Ellens, & Ryan, 1999; McMinn, Ellens, & Soref, 1999; Michaels, 2006). One way that some report writers deal with this is to qualify their "interpretations" by stating something like "People with these types of profiles. . . ." The problem here is that for the reader it implies that the "interpretations" are indeed accurate portrayals of the person. Probably most referral sources would be disappointed if they knew that much of the time only about half the "interpretations" accurately describe the person that they have referred for assessment. For example, if a client were to have a mild to moderate elevation on an MMPI-2 scale, the report writer might be tempted to list the various descriptors for that elevation. Whereas many of these descriptors might be accurate for someone scoring quite high, the accuracy for mild to moderate elevations is much less. Some report writers might take this into account by toning down the descriptors, thereby helping to increase the accuracy. However, this still does not mean that the clinician has then determined which of the toned-down descriptors are accurate versus those that are false.

A further reason not to present interpretations test-by-test is that the "interpretations" may contradict results from other sources of information. When the results are listed test-by-test, these contradictions are rarely taken into account. There may be a wide number of reasons for contradictions among sources of assessment information including client deception, differing results due to self-report as opposed to performance-based measures, ethnic/cultural factors, or the client taking some of the tests during states that do not represent their typical level of functioning (see the Impressions and Interpretations section in Chapter 3).

Despite the rationale for presenting interpretations according to functional domains rather than test-by-test, the PRWA does include the option of customizing report templates. This feature allows report writers to develop their own templates that could include organizing interpretations in a test-by-test format. This acknowledges that some report writers may still prefer the test-by-test approach since they may feel this is best for teaching purposes, is consistent with how they have become accustomed to writing reports, and provides a clear association where the inferences were derived from. However, this would mean that some of the PRWA Wizards developed for functional domains (e.g., common phrases for abilities, personality, etc.) will not be available.

The essence of the approach advocated in this book and associated software program is for clinicians to integrate their assessment information *before* they present their interpretations. The PRWA provides various tools to facilitate this process. The grid format described previously and illustrated in Figure 2.1 will help clinicians to organize and integrate their interpretations before they write them in the various functional domains of the Impressions and Interpretations section. Sometimes, however, clinicians are advised to detail why they came to certain interpretations or opinions. This is particularly the case with forensic evaluations. The PRWA allows report writers to summarize and then easily view their notes for an interpretation or opinion included in the Integrated Information Manager that would then allow them to easily track, support, and then describe how they arrived at their interpretations/opinions. For example, if the interpretation was for poor executive functioning, clinicians might write something like "Based on low scores on the NAB executive functioning module, reports from informants, and behavioral observations, Mr. Jones has a mild impairment in his executive functioning." However, for most referral contexts, detailing the clinician's reasoning processes would not be advised since it would likely be unnecessary, needlessly increase the length of a report, and be distracting to most readers.

A component of the search included in the PRWA helps report writers to identify when they might have presented their interpretations in a test-by-test, unintegrated manner. When a phrase is identified that suggests a test-oriented style, the phrase would be highlighted. Possible phrases might be ". . . people with this code type are described as . . ." or ". . . scores on the MMPI-2 indicate. . . ." The information would explain the rationale for why the phrase might be problematic and then offer suggestions on how the interpretations might be worked with differently. For example, if a report writer wrote "*People with these profiles . . .*" the explanatory information would read:

> This phrase suggests minimal integration in that there is a focus on a "profile" rather than the person. It also suggests that there has not been an integration of all the sources of data in developing the interpretations. Your referral source is probably not so much interested in "people with these types of profiles," but with whether or not a specific descriptor accurately describes the person being assessed. In addition, a simple listing of various possible descriptors without determining if they are accurate or not is likely to result in a number of inaccurate descriptors. Your referral source will not be able to determine which of these are accurate, yet, by you listing them, it implies that they are accurately describing your client. One situation in which it may be necessary to discuss "people with these profiles" would be forensic reports in which the clinician

may need to be more guarded about what he or she says and may need to more closely adhere to both test scores as well as the reasoning they used to come to his or her final opinions. SUGGESTIONS: Consider all sources of information and, once the interpretations have been given sufficient support, go directly to making interpretations. State something like "Mr. Smith typically copes with stress by . . ." rather than "People with these profiles cope with stress by. . . ."

## 4. Minimal Reference to Tests and Testing

The extent to which report writers refer to tests and test scores varies widely (see Groth-Marnat & Horvath, 2006). On the one extreme are clinicians who don't include test scores in the body of the report itself, nor do they include them as an appendix. A moderate use of scores can be found with clinicians who occasionally refer to scores in their interpretations and provide a full listing of scores as an appendix. At the other extreme are report writers who insert scores liberally both in their interpretations and include all relevant test scores either in a test results section in the body of the report itself or in an appendix.

Professional psychologists who advocate the extensive insertion of test scores in reports point out that it allows readers to follow how the report writer came to their conclusions. This may be particularly important in legal settings where clinicians need to document and be held accountable for their opinions. Because the data are readily available, the need for legal discovery of relevant information related to the client is reduced. Providing actual data also gives a report a precise, scientific feel. Qualified professionals can also use the data to make comparisons with other evaluations that either have been done or might be done in the future. For example, including test scores might allow a treatment team to track improvement in cognitive functioning, or a reduction in depression might be tracked over several different assessments.

There are also professional psychologists who advocate minimizing the extent to which test scores are included and referred to. The most frequent reason cited is that test scores may be misinterpreted (Pieniadz & Kelland, 2001). This may occur by qualified professionals who may look at a score and make incorrect inferences because they do not have access to the full range of assessment information such as behavioral observations or medical/vocational records that the report writer might have used. Misinterpretations might also occur by nonqualified persons or the client him- or herself. For example, a client might misinterpret the meaning of his IQ scores, or he might note that he has a mild to moderate elevation on a scale called "mania" and think this means that the tests found he was "manic."

Freedom-of-information legislation means that it is quite likely that clients will obtain copies of their reports. This increases the chances that if they have the actual scores, they might be harmed if the scores are misinterpreted. However, the 2002 APA ethics code (American Psychological Association [APA] Committee on Professional Practice and Standards, 2002) does give clients the right to both see their own test scores and decide whom the scores will be given to. This means that report writers need to balance a client's right to have his or her test scores with the potential for harm to the client. One way of minimizing potential harm is to include a minimal number of test scores in the report. If the client specifically requests that they be released, then it is incumbent on the clinician to minimize the potential for harm by explaining the scores both to the person they will be sent to and to the client him- or herself.

A further reason to minimize the inclusion of test scores is that the extensive reference to scores can result in reports that sound like they are more focused on tests and test scores rather than the person and the world that the client lives in. This can result in a cluttered, mechanistic view of the person. Whereas report writers should use the best of what's known regarding the technical side of testing, the results should also describe the person. This should include describing the client's experience of their world, using professional but everyday language, and placing the assessment results into the larger context of the client's life.

As a result of the preceding considerations, the PRWA software encourages clinicians to minimize their reference to tests and test scores. This is facilitated by guidelines, sample reports, and common phrases that minimize reference to test scores. An important tool for minimizing test-oriented language also occurs when alerts appear when software users activate the scan ("red flag") function to identify possible problematic language. Highly test-oriented language identified by the scan function may include such phrases as ". . . a high score on . . ." or ". . . the 15-point difference between. . . ." Following is a sample alert with a

RAPID REFERENCE 2.3: REASONS FOR AND AGAINST
INCLUDING TEST SCORES

*Reasons to minimize test scores:*

- Reduces misinterpretation by both professionals and clients
- Reduces potential for client harm
- Enhances a person-oriented presentation (rather than a test-oriented presentation)
- Increases readability

*Reasons to emphasize test scores:*

- Links data with interpretations
- Precise, scientific appearance
- Provides data points for past/future reference

rationale and suggestions that would result when the report writer writes "... the low score of ...":

> This suggests a test-oriented description and minimal integration of results. It also suggests that you are focusing on the "scores" rather than the person. In other words, there has not been an integration of all relevant sources of data in developing your interpretations. It also suggests you might be spending too much time detailing your reasoning process. SUGGESTION: Provide interpretations based on convergence of various sources of information, avoid reference to the specific score, and avoid detailing your reasoning processes.

Although the PRWA encourages report writers to minimize their reference to tests and test scores, there are times when the strong inclusion of test scores is important. The most obvious situation is when a qualified person has requested an evaluation and specifically requested that test scores be provided. A possible reason to have the scores might be to monitor changes in a client's condition. In certain situations where maximum accountability is required, it might also be advisable to more directly link interpretations/opinions to test scores. This is particularly likely to occur in forensic and educational settings. The extent of test scores may vary according to which tests were used. IQ/index scores on the WAIS-IV/ WISC-IV are quite easy to give, and there are resources to assist report readers in understanding what they mean. In contrast, Rorschach scores are quite numerous, opaque, and filled with technical language (e.g., "lambda" or "erlebnistypus"). As a result, report writers should be more hesitant to include scores from the Rorschach. However, the decision to release test scores should always be based on balancing various ethical requirements, client rights, potential harm, test security, and copyright laws.

## 5. INTEGRATED/READABLE EXPANSION OF INTERPRETATIONS THAT ARE CONNECTED TO CLIENT'S WORLD

The consistent theme of the PRWA as well as the *Handbook of Psychological Assessment* (5th edition) is integrating assessment information. Core strategies 1, 3, and 6 all have this as a common theme. One major integrative strategy is integrating all sources of assessment information in order to make interpretations that are then organized according to functional domains (see core strategy 3). Not only should test results be integrated with other relevant test scores, but the test results should also be integrated with behavioral observations, background information, client records, and descriptions provided by informants. The clinician should strive to understand possible contradictions among sources of data (see the Impressions and Interpretations section in Chapter 3). An ideal paragraph might include interpretations that begin as general statements, proceed to more specific interpretations, include descriptions of representative testing behaviors, and finally, include information on how the person would do on relevant everyday behaviors. Resources in the PRWA allow report writers to organize this information in preparation for writing subsections for various functional domains (see core strategy 3).

Two other levels of integration are included in core strategies 1 and 6. Integration within the report itself can be enhanced by the referral questions being numbered in the Referral Question section, and then these questions can be answered in the Summary and Recommendations section (core strategy 1). The numbering in the Referral Question section should correspond with the numbers of the referral questions that are answered in the Summary section. A final aspect of integration is to make sure that the recommendations are not only specific and concrete, but are also integrated with actual resources in the community and correspond to what clients themselves believe they can and would like to do (core strategy 6). The recommendations can begin with a statement of what they should address followed by the recommendation itself ("*In order to reduce Ms. Smith's level of anxiety*, it is recommended that she practice 20 minutes of mindfulness-based meditation twice a day . . .").

---

### RAPID REFERENCE 2.4: AREAS OF INTEGRATION

- Integrate referral questions and summary through coordinated numbering.
- Use functional domains.
- Integrate relevant sources of information: test scores, history, behavioral observations, informant reports, records (medical, academic, legal, occupational).
- Resolve contradictions among data.
- Include different levels of interpretation: general statement, specific subcomponents, qualitative descriptions of test responses, examples from history, behavioral observations, implications for everyday life.
- Integrate recommendations with assessment information, best practices, client/referral acceptance, community resources.

---

## 6. RECOMMENDATIONS SUFFICIENTLY BROAD, TREATMENT PLAN INTEGRATED WITH INTERPRETATIONS, RELATED TO CLIENT'S WORLD

Consumers of psychological reports consistently rate the recommendations as the single most useful section (Brenner, 2003). Guidelines and a format for recommendations are given in Chapters 3 and 4. In addition, the PRWA provides menus for creating recommendations tailored to the different types of reports. The most important guidelines for recommendations are that they should be pragmatic and concrete. They should also be informed by best practices guidelines (American Psychological Association, www.apa.org/practice/prof.html; American Psychiatric Association:

www.psychiatryonline.com/pracGuide/pracGuideTopic_9.aspx; Society of Clinical Psychology: www.psychologicaltreatments.org). A further strategy is that they should also be linked to available resources in the community as well as be options that the referral source and the client him- or herself would be likely to actually follow. For example, a client with minimal education and with cognitive impairment would be unlikely to follow through on recommendations for them to use self-help online resources. Problematic recommendations occur when they are too general, abstract, and do not connect to available resources in the community. Another area of potential difficulty is when report writers include too many recommendations. This is likely to overwhelm the reader with too many options such that they may not end up following any of the suggestions provided. Built in to the PRWA scan for problematic ("red flag") phrases are alerts that identify when report writers might have included too many recommendations. Report writers can then note the alert, reflect on the number of recommendations they have included, and then decide whether to modify the number of recommendation they have written.

RAPID REFERENCE 2.5: GUIDELINES FOR RECOMMENDATIONS

- Pragmatic and concrete
- Informed by best practices
- Link to community resources
- Options the referral source and client will be likely to follow
- Provide a moderate number

# Recommended Reading

Armengol, C. G., Kaplan, E., & Moes, E. J. (Eds.). (2001). *The consumer-oriented neuropsychological report.* Lutz, FL: Psychological Assessment Resources.

Brenner, E. (2003). Consumer-focused psychological assessment. *Professional Psychology: Research and Practice, 34,* 240–247.

Grisso, T. (2010). Guidance for improving forensic reports: A review of common errors. *Open Access Journal of Forensic Psychology, 2,* 102–115; www.forensicpsychologyunbound.ws/-2010.2:233-240

Groth-Marnat, G. & Horvath, L. S. (2006). The psychological report: A review of current controversies. *Journal of Clinical Psychology, 62,* 73–81.

Groth-Marnat, G. (2009b). The five assessment issues you meet when you go to heaven. *Journal of Personality Assessment, 91,* 303–310.

Harvey, V. S. (2006). Variables affecting the clarity of reports. *Journal of Clinical Psychology, 62,* 5–18.

Pieniadz, J., & Kelland, D. Z. (2001). Reporting scores in neuropsychological assessment: Ethical, validity, practicality, and more. In C. G. Armengol, E. Kaplan, & E. J. Moes (Eds.), *The consumer-oriented neuropsychological report* (pp. 123–140). Lutz, FL: Psychological Assessment Resources.

# CHAPTER 3

# Format of the Psychological Report

One of the earliest and most important considerations for writing a psychological report is deciding on its structure. Although there are many variations, they all have the following 10 components:

1. Identifying information
2. Referral question
3. Evaluation procedures
4. Behavioral observations/mental status
5. Background information
6. Test results
7. Impressions and interpretations
8. Summary
9. Recommendations
10. Signature/title

The above format is the core for the Psychological Report Writing Assistant (PRWA) as well as this chapter. Much of the information included in this chapter is derived from Groth-Marnat (2009a) as well as Goldfinger and Pomerantz (2010); Lichtenberger, Mather, Kaufman, and Kaufman (2004); and Sattler (2008). As a result, the chapter synthesizes standard information on the structure and content of the psychological report. At the same time, it should be noted that professional psychologists often vary from this format. For example, sometimes a separate heading is used for the history of the presenting problem or for mental status. Often, the setting and type of report will require slightly different headings from those listed above. For example, forensic reports often include a separate section for the validity of the results and for review of records. Although the PRWA uses the format described above, it also includes sufficient flexibility so that report writers can insert their own sections and subsections into their reports as needed.

The PRWA program leads the report writer through the various sections of the psychological report. In some cases there are components of the software that can streamline the process. For example, in the Evaluation Procedures section, the report writer simply places a check in the box to the left of the test, clicks "insert into text," and the test will automatically appear in the body of the report. In addition, there are common phrases that can help the report writer edit common phrases used in psychological reports (e.g., "Mr. Smith's overall intellectual ability was in the _____ range [Full Scale IQ = ___, __ percentile]). The Summary and Recommendations portion of the software also has a menu of possible recommendations that can automatically be inserted into the report by checking the box to the left of the recommendation, and then clicking "insert into text."

One crucial feature of the PRWA is that it has developed formats, guidelines, and tools to assist report writers in developing the following types of reports:

Cognitive
Neuropsychological
Psychoeducational
Personality
Forensic

Separating the reports into different report modules was considered essential in that each type of report has different requirements that need to be incorporated into the content and structure of the report (see Chapter 5). For example, neuropsychological reports need to pay particular attention to a client's medical and academic/social history. The Impressions and Interpretations section also needs to have subheadings relevant for domains frequently considered in organizing a person's neuropsychological functioning (i.e., memory and learning, verbal functioning, speed of processing, visual-spatial/perceptual functioning, executive functioning). In contrast, a vocational report would have subheadings that would organize a person's functioning according to abilities, interests, and personality. The various types of reports also have different menus for selecting possible recommendations.

Each of the 10 sections of a psychological report requires different content. Some of this content is mandatory, such as the name of the person being evaluated, whereas other information is determined by the requirements of the referral question and the various findings of the professional psychologist. The remainder of this chapter provides guidelines for how to complete each of the sections. These sections are also included in the PRWA software. Accordingly, this chapter also provides information on and a guide to working with the tools and resources that have been integrated into the software program.

## IDENTIFYING INFORMATION

This is one of the most structured, "fill-in-the-blanks" sections of the report in that it requires the report writer to include the name of the client, his date of birth, date of evaluation, who referred him, and the name of the examiner along with his or her title. Psychoeducational reports on children and adolescents often have report writers include the school and grade the clients are in. The PRWA lists each of these components so that the report writer merely needs to fill in the required information. This is then automatically inserted into the body of the report.

## REFERRAL QUESTION

The referral question section introduces the reader to essential features of the client and explains why the client is there and what questions need to be asked. It thus provides the focus for the rest of the report. It is not at all unusual for the referral source to not have a clear conception of how to ask the referral questions. Sometimes the questions are much too vague, or they cannot be realistically answered by psychological assessment. Sometimes there are hidden agendas that need to be uncovered, with the result that formal testing may not even be the optimal means of addressing the problem. This means that clinicians will often need to work with the referral source to clarify the referral questions. One of the best ways to accomplish this goal is to ask the referral source what decisions they need to make regarding the client. This information can then be integrated into how the questions are phrased.

At the very least, the referral question section should include three components. The first should be an orienting sentence that describes the age, ethnicity, relationship/marital status, and gender of the person who has been evaluated. Neuropsychological/cognitive evaluations should also include the handedness of the person because this can have implications for risk factors. For example, persons who are left-handed have a greater incidence of learning disabilities, have somewhat better recoveries following an acquired brain injury, and their speech centers may be located in the right hemisphere. The second component should include a brief listing of the complaints that explain why the person is being evaluated ("Ms. Client reported that she has been experiencing irritability, feelings of helplessness, reduced appetite, and difficulty staying asleep"). The final component should list the questions that need to be answered. It is recommended that the questions be numbered. The numbers and corresponding referral questions can then be answered in the Summary and Recommendations section (also see core strategy 1 in Chapter 2). This provides symmetry, readability, and closure to the report. Two examples of a referral question section are as follows:

> Mr. Jones is a 70-year-old, European American, married, right-handed male with 12 years of education who was referred due to self-reported concerns with his memory. Complaints include not being able to recall the names of people, missing meetings, forgetting the time, difficulty recalling which day it is, stress, and anxiety. My understanding is that the following questions need to be answered:
>
> 1. What is the magnitude of his memory and other cognitive difficulties?
> 2. What diagnostic possibilities might his pattern of cognitive abilities suggest?
> 3. What recommendations seem appropriate?

or

> Ms. Personality is a 47-year-old, divorced, European American female with 16 years of education who has been experiencing difficulties with alcohol, loneliness, and depression. Self-reported complaints include feeling tired, having difficulty sleeping, and binge drinking. Specific questions that need to be addressed are the following:

1. What is the role her personality plays in her alcohol-related difficulties?
2. What are the characteristics most relevant for developing a treatment plan?
3. What would be an optimal treatment plan?

Both of the preceding examples follow the three-component format. In some cases, it might be advisable to include additional detail, especially related to complaints and previous assessment or treatment. However, this should be done cautiously since there is a danger that the Referral Question section could become too long. The bulk of the history regarding the person should be included in the Background Information section. A further guideline is that only information crucial to orienting the reader to the purpose of the evaluation and the questions that need to be answered should be included. In addition, the referral questions should be stated succinctly and should be able to be answered. Keep in mind that the purpose of a psychological evaluation is to solve problems. Thus, the original questions should be articulated in such a way that they can realistically be expected to assist in this goal.

## EVALUATION PROCEDURES

The Evaluation Procedures section is simply a listing of which procedures were used to evaluate the client. This consists primarily of listing the tests that were administered. The tests should be written out with their full names followed by their abbreviations (e.g., "Wechsler Adult Intelligence Scale–IV [WAIS-IV]"). The interview should also be included along with the degree of structure (e.g., "semistructured clinical interview"). This section should also list any other procedures such as review of medical, school, personnel, or military records. If relevant, the person who wrote the record and the date of the record should also be included. Sometimes classroom or work behaviors are made, and the date of these behaviors needs to be included. The final portion of the evaluation procedures is usually a phrase indicating the total face-to-face length of the evaluation.

The PRWA resources include lists of tests and other procedures that frequently occur for the different types of reports. For example, personality reports will include such instruments as the MMPI-2/MMPI-2-RF, Psychological Assessment Inventory, or the NEO-PI-3. In contrast, psychoeducational reports will be more likely to include the Wechsler Intelligence Scale for Children–IV, Woodcock Johnson–III, Connor's Teacher Rating Scale Revised–Long Form, and classroom observations. The user of the program simply needs to indicate which of the instruments were used, and they can then be automatically inserted into the body of the report. In the event that a procedure is not listed, the report writer can type in the additional instrument in the composition window of the report.

## BEHAVIORAL OBSERVATIONS/MENTAL STATUS

Behavioral observations can assist the overall assessment process by supplementing the findings from other procedures, providing examples of behaviors the test finding will later explain, and providing information related to the validity of the assessment results. Behaviors are generally based on what the clinician actually observes. Interpretations regarding the behavior should be avoided. For example, instead of stating that the client was "moderately depressed," the clinician should state something like ". . . eye contact was minimal, speech was slow, and they sometimes made self-critical statements such as 'You must think I'm pretty stupid.'" The time to conclude that the client was "moderately depressed" will be in the Impressions and Interpretations and the Summary sections.

As previously noted, behavioral observations can often provide a useful supplement to other assessment findings. For example, if a person does score high on formal measures of depression, then the behavioral observations can provide an introduction to and useful information on how the depression is expressed. Thus, the behavioral observations can provide a useful strategy to help give the feel of the person. This means that the clinician needs to pay close attention to which behaviors to identify and insert into the behavioral observations. As previously noted, using actual quotes can sometimes be an effective means of recording relevant behavioral observations.

A further function of behavioral observations is to introduce the reader to the problem behavior that will later be expanded in the rest of the report. For example, a client presenting with cognitive complaints will often demonstrate many of these difficulties during the interview or testing. They may have difficulty finding the right word, demonstrate concrete thinking, behave in a slow manner, need to be given considerable direction, have problems with memory, be distractible, or have little insight into their behavior. Each of these behaviors represents an opportunity for the clinician to describe them and then expand on the various difficulties in later portions of the report.

A final general purpose of the Behavioral Observations section is that it can potentially provide information relevant to assessing the accuracy of the findings. Some clients work hard, stay focused, and appear to give their best efforts to the tasks presented to them. In contrast, others might appear unmotivated and not appear to take the tasks particularly seriously. Clients who are malingering might reflect on their responses, suggesting that they are carefully monitoring their responses. These and other, similar behaviors can help to make conclusions related to the accuracy of the overall assessment results.

The topics included in the behavioral observations section are typically related to the following areas:

Appearance
Examiner–client interaction
Physical appearance
Level of cooperation/motivation
Mood and affect
Thought processes

These topics can potentially result in quite long descriptions of the client's behavior. This means that one of the skills of the report writer is to summarize the behaviors in a concise manner. Usually, behavioral observations are summarized in a single paragraph. Sometimes, however, the behaviors are an extremely rich source of information and need to be described in two to three paragraphs. One guideline to help make the behavioral observations concise is to include only those behaviors that are unique and informative. Stating that the person was of average height and dressed "appropriately" would not be likely to provide useful information. In contrast, describing the unusual clothes a client wore and that he was extremely tall might be quite useful in expanding the understanding of the client.

Often, the client's mental status is an important part of behavioral observations. This typically begins with a statement summarizing his orientation to the assessment process ("Mr. Jones was oriented to person, time, place, and reason for evaluation"). This is particularly important for inpatient intakes, where there may be some question regarding whether the client is fully oriented. In contrast, including a statement regarding orientation in outpatient counseling settings is less important, and this should only rarely be done for vocational assessments. In addition to orientation, mental status also includes information related to mood/affect and thought processes ("The client had a flat affect throughout the assessment, but on two occasions he cried. There was no evidence of delusions or hallucination, but insight was poor and thought processes were concrete."). Often, verbalizations, psychomotor activity, and insight/judgment are also noted and described. Sometimes, particularly in psychiatric settings, a description of mental status is quite extensive and is a major portion of the evaluation. As a result, it is sometimes developed as a section that is separate from the Behavioral Observations.

It is customary at the end of the Behavioral Observations section to include a statement related to the validity of the assessment results. If there is good evidence that the results are valid, then a brief sentence is all that's needed ("Given the above behavioral observations and pattern of test results, the findings appear to be an accurate assessment of the person's current level of functioning."). However, if the results are questionable, then further elaboration is often needed ("Given observations of the client's behavior combined with the results of tests developed to identify poor effort, the results are likely to be a significant underestimate of the client's optimal level of functioning. The reason for this is . . ."). This is particularly crucial in forensic settings, where it is often important to include an entire section devoted to describing the validity of the assessment results.

## BACKGROUND INFORMATION

The Background Information section introduces the client to the reader, provides a context for the rest of the report, and includes information that is often crucial for interpretations regarding the client. It is usually divided into various domains (personal/social, academic, legal, medical). The Background Information section is also sometimes labeled Relevant History, Relevant Information, or Background/History.

In most cases, the majority of the information will be derived from interviewing the client him- or herself. Some of this information will include facts (e.g., number of siblings), but in other cases it may involve the client's impressions of work or family relationships (e.g., ". . . the client stated that there was continuous tension among family members . . ."). Sometimes a quote can nicely capture the client's perception of a person, event, or situation ("I've hated most of the jobs I've had . . ."). Most reports include at least some outside information. This means clinicians will need to interview persons such as parents, spouses, children, employers, or teachers. In some cases, outside sources will be crucial. This is particularly the case when the client is a poor or questionable historian. For example, evaluations of children will rely quite heavily on information provided by the parents and possibly teachers. Legal evaluations will also rely quite heavily on various legal, medical, and employment records. This is in part to confirm (or disconfirm) the narrative of events that the client has provided. Due to the wide number of potential sources of information, it is essential to designate where the information came from. Sample phrases are ". . . the client reported that . . ." or ". . . the medical report by Dr. Smith (dated March 22, 2014) concluded that . . . ."

Report writers need to be sensitive to the possible impact information might have on the client or other persons described in the report. For example, information regarding family-related illegal activity, substance abuse, or medical problems may not be appropriate. This is especially the case for a forensic evaluation that has the potential to become part of the public domain. In some cases, however, including this type of information may be crucial to answering the referral questions. A further example of potentially problematic information might be past diagnoses that have been given to the client. This is particularly important for diagnoses such as borderline personality disorder, antisocial personality disorder, bipolar disorder, or schizophrenia. These may result in readers of the report developing negative impressions of the client at an early stage. Moderating factors might be that these diagnoses were inaccurate. In addition, there is quite wide variability in the degree to which clients have resolved and adjusted to mental health problems, but a label may not adequately reflect these differences. This means that report writers need to carefully balance the importance of the information with the potential for the information to cause harm to the client or persons described in the Background Information section.

The length of the Background Information section can vary depending on the preference of the report writer, context it is written in, and the extent that it is needed to make the report complete. Some authors recommend that it be limited to one paragraph. This is particularly the case in medical settings where being concise is crucial. Having said this, it is sometimes the case where a more extensive history written for a referral from a physician can be extremely valuable. More typically, the Background Information section organizes the information around four to five domains with one paragraph for each of the domains. This means that the total length varies from half to a maximum of one and a half single-spaced pages. Report writers should, however, be cautious not to expand the Background Information section so that it dominates the rest of the report.

The PRWA program uses the following domains: personal/social, academic/vocational, medical, and mental health. Other common domains are legal history or history of the problem. However, the history of the problem is usually sufficiently covered by the brief introduction in the Referral Question section combined with information provided in the medical and/or mental health sections. The amount of information included in each domain depends largely on the purpose of the report. A cognitive/neuropsychological evaluation will need to focus on medical and academic/vocational information. In contrast, a personality evaluation will focus more on family, personal, and mental health history.

The personal/social subsection should begin with a brief introduction into the client's background (". . . Ms. Jones was born in a rural section of northern Idaho and lived there until the age of 18. Her parents were . . ."). A personality evaluation will typically provide some degree of depth into the client's family history because this is so crucial in understanding what led into their personality and possible psychological difficulties. This often includes such things as whether their parents stayed married or were divorced, as well as the relationship the client had with his or her parents and siblings. How many siblings did the client have? Is the client single, married, or divorced? Do they have children and, if so, how many and what are their ages? Are the parents alive or deceased? If they are alive, what is their current and past health status? What was the parent's socioeconomic status, and what did they do for work? What was the family's cultural background and identity? It is often helpful to know the emotional atmosphere of the family and if there were any major events that defined the client's relationship with his or her family.

Academic/vocational history allows the reader of the report to understand the client's level of and possible problems with school and work. Early school recall by the client is likely to be vague but can often reveal the client's perception of important formative events. What were the client's relationships with his or her peers and teachers? What were their best and worst subjects, and what were their grades like? Was there any indication of learning problems, attentional difficulties, or problems with conduct? Many of the academic/personal memories become more accurate when recounting information related to high school. In some cases, it might be important to obtain actual school records. This is especially the case when trying to understand learning problems or to provide objective evidence of a client's premorbid level of functioning. It is also important to understand how the client entered the workforce, what jobs he has done, his level of satisfaction, and how his career has changed over time.

As noted previously, medical history is particularly important for cognitive/neuropsychological reports. In order to better understand the client's current level of functioning, it is necessary to screen for possible preexisting conditions including learning disabilities, head injuries, unusually high fevers, strokes, or exposure to neurotoxic substances including alcohol, recreational drugs, or industrial toxins (e.g., lead, mercury, styrene). It is not unusual for a current event to occur, such as a head injury, but then understanding the impact of this injury can be complicated by a preexisting learning disability combined with chronic use of alcohol. If a head injury has occurred, it is important to determine whether the client was unconscious, the duration of the possible loss of consciousness, whether she recalls details related to the injury itself, the last memory prior to the injury, the first thing she recalled following the injury, and the time that has elapsed from the moment she lost consciousness to her first memory. These details can assist in determining the seriousness of the head injury and give a rough indication of the extent of postinjury complications. More general medical history is also important to cover. This should include any illnesses she has had and current medications the client is taking. It is not unusual for medical conditions and drug interactions to result in psychological problems. These problems may be most effectively addressed through medical rather than purely psychological interventions.

The mental health subsection includes the client's history of personal difficulties or psychological distress. Thus, things such as personal struggles, shyness, grief, loneliness, distress, or mild depression might be areas to include. In many cases, a client's difficulties might have become severe enough to be considered psychiatric disorders. In these cases, it would be important to describe the full nature of the symptoms. Thus, it would be important to not only state that the client was "depressed" but to also elaborate on how the depression is or had been expressed. In a case of depression, this may include somatic features such as low energy, reduced appetite, sleep disturbance, gastrointestinal complaints, anhedonia, or slowed thinking processes. Features may also include thoughts of hopelessness, a sense of helplessness, self-critical thoughts, flat affect, or irritability. In addition, to including the nature of a disorder, it would also be important to include its onset, duration, frequency (if appropriate), and intensity. The preceding comprehensive description not only serves the purpose of covering essential aspects of the person, but also assists in supporting any diagnosis that might be included in the Summary section. In other words, the report writer needs to carefully consider whether the specific *Diagnostic and Statistical Manual of Mental Disorders*, 5th Edition (*DSM-5*) criteria do or do not match the symptom the client presents with.

A particular issue report writers need to contend with is whether the information is sufficiently comprehensive. A common error is to only focus on the first and most obvious set of complaints that the client presents with. Since comorbid conditions are quite common, it may be essential to also investigate further to determine if there are other difficulties. This is particularly the case when these may be relatively hidden problems such as dissociation. In addition, many clinicians may feel hesitant to explore sexual dysfunction and substance abuse. This may be combined with resistance on the part of the client to discuss these issues. It may be even more problematic if the client either believes he does not have a problem (even when other sources indicate he does) or wants to actively hide that the problem exists. This frequently occurs with substance abuse and anorexia nervosa.

A final feature of the mental health section is to determine past and current treatment. Has the client been in psychotherapy, undergone rehabilitation, or taken psychoactive medication? If he or she is currently taking psychoactive medication, then what type, for how long, and what is his or her current dose? It would also be important to determine the client's attitude toward treatment and outcome of any treatments that have been administered.

Clearly, the preceding information is potentially quite extensive. As a result, a potential problem is that report writers might be overly inclusive such that the Background Information section becomes too long and dominates the report. In order to work with this, report writers should always keep in mind what is essential to include versus which information is extraneous and can thus be excluded. At the same time, report writers should make sure that all essential information has indeed been covered.

## TEST RESULTS

The Test Results section summarizes the actual scores the client received. Any scores should be given as standard scores and not raw scores. This is simply because raw scores won't be understood by the reader. If available, it is also important to include percentiles to accompany the standard scores. This is because percentiles are probably the most easily understood way to communicate the meaning of the scores for both professionals and untrained persons. Clarity can be further enhanced by stating something like ". . . Mr. Jones scored in the 5th percentile, which means that only 5% of the population scored lower than him." It is also good to designate the relative magnitude of selected scores by stating next to them whether the score was mild, moderate, or highly elevated or lowered. Wechsler intelligence subtests can also be listed with their standard scores ($M = 10$, $SD = 3$) and, if appropriate, a designation can be given as to whether they represent strengths ("S") or weaknesses ("W").

The preceding guidelines for test scores are fairly straightforward for norm-based instruments such as the WAIS-IV/Wechsler Intelligence Scale for Children–IV (WISC-IV) and the Minnesota Multiphasic Personality Inventory (MMPI-2/MMPI-2-RF). When displaying the results of performance-based personality instruments (often referred to as *projectives*) summarizing the results becomes more problematic. The entire Rorschach summary sheet can be given, but it is then not clear what represents a high or low score. This may change as the Rorschach-Performance Assessment System (Meyer, Viglione, Mihura, Erard, & Erdberg, 2011) becomes used more extensively because it includes graphical presentation of the data. At the present time, and when using the Comprehensive System, report writers might simply place "high," "extremely high," "low," and so on next to scores of interest. Instruments such as the Thematic Apperception Test (TAT) or Human Figure Drawings might provide a brief narrative summarizing the results by stating something like "TAT results indicated stories with themes of rejection, anger, and pessimism. . . ."

There is considerable variation on how best to present test results (see Groth-Marnat & Horvath, 2006). Many report writers prefer not to include any test results unless specifically asked to do so. In these cases, they might simply state in the Test Results section something like "Test scores are available upon request." At the other extreme are report writers who list as many of the scores as possible and combine this with extensive inclusion of the scores in the Impressions and Interpretations section. An intermediate approach is to provide an appendix that includes the scores. The PRWA includes a menu that opens up a series of options for listing scores for many of the more frequently used tests. The extent to which test scores are included will depend on the setting of the report, preferences of the referral source, training of the referral source, personal preference of the report writer, and the policy at the agency where the report is being written.

## IMPRESSIONS AND INTERPRETATIONS (OR SIMPLY "FINDINGS" FOR FORENSIC REPORTS)

This section is typically one of the most important but also the most difficult section to write. As a result, numerous tools are available in the PRWA to help organize, integrate, and expand a report writer's interpretations. This includes guidelines, examples, strategies for integrating test results, links to move the writer to different sections of the report, and a search function that alerts report writers to the possibility that problematic phrases have been used. It is anticipated that this will lead the report writer through the various sections in a way that is natural to their thinking and provides them with useful resources to assist in the process.

The various topics in the Impressions and Interpretations section should be organized according to domains (Ms. Smith's verbal abilities were in the . . ."). In contrast, a strategy in which report writers present the results test-by-test is discouraged (see core strategy 3 in Chapter 2). Despite this, PRWA users do have the option of customizing reports, and this may include developing a test-by-test format. If a functional domain approach is selected, it will vary according to the referral question and the type of report (see Chapter 5). For example, a neuropsychological report would most likely include subsections according to attention, language, spatial abilities, memory, and executive functions. In contrast, a vocational report would be more likely to include discussions of the client's abilities, interests, and personality. As a result, the listing of possible domains in the PRWA varies according to the type of report the clinician is writing. At the same time, the PRWA is flexible in that clinicians can easily add their own categories and number of new domains into the report composition screen.

## Using the Integrated Information Manager

Perhaps the most crucial task in writing interpretations is to organize the assessment information in such a way that the report writer can easily extract the relevant interpretations. PRWA helps the report writer to accomplish this goal by providing an information manager that allows report writers to summarize, organize, and integrate the various sources of information (see Chapter 2, Figure 2.1, p. 23 for a sample abbreviated grid from of the Integrated Information Manager). The manager is arranged in a grid fashion such that the domains that will be used to organize the Impressions and Interpretations section are listed in the lower column on the left side of the grid (e.g., verbal abilities, coping style). The row at the top of the grid lists the sources of information (e.g., WAIS-IV, MMPI-2, MCMI-III, behavioral observations) that will be used to inform the domain. For example, a clinician may be interested in describing a client's verbal abilities. They would begin by noting the "verbal abilities" domain listed on the top of the grid and then noting the various sources of information to the left of the grid. Report writers can enlarge each of the relevant domain X source by placing the cursor into the box and clicking. This will allow the report writer more space to make notes. For example, the WAIS-IV might have resulted in a high score on the Verbal Comprehension Index. This can be noted along with what a high score might mean (". . . good word knowledge, large fund of general knowledge, ability to articulate thoughts . . ."). The clinician may next note relevant behavioral observations. These might confirm that the client appeared to have a good vocabulary and excellent verbal fluency. However, the clinician might also have noted that the client used an excessive number of words, included a large number of details, and seemed quite tangential. The Millon Clinical Multiaxial Inventory–III (MCMI-III) might indicate that the person scored quite high on being compulsive. This further expands the understanding of the client's verbal abilities in that he or she was extremely concerned with details and tried to be perfectionistic. When the report writer composes the paragraph on verbal abilities, he or she can draw on and organize the various sources of information.

The Integrated Information Manager can be used to both document the basis for inferences regarding the client and make notes for writing the domain-based interpretations. If a report writer is mainly concerned with documenting where the inferences came from, he or she can include actual data. In the verbal abilities example provided above, the WAIS-IV Verbal Comprehension Index score can be inserted ("WAIS-IV VCI = 126") along with the relevant MCMI-III score ("MCMI-III [7] Compulsive = 86"). This may be particularly important for a forensic or other types of reports where clinicians may need to be accountable for why they made their interpretations. However, simply listing the data may not be particularly helpful in developing a narrative related to the client. A narrative would be easiest to write if report writers first list brief phrases related to the relevant domain in the relevant grids for the Integrated Information Manager. The WAIS-IV box might then contain phrases such as "excellent verbal abilities, good fund of knowledge, excellent vocabulary, good common sense reasoning." In addition, the MCMI-III box might include "focus on details, perfectionistic, describes information from multiple perspectives." These and other phrases can then be combined to quite easily create a coherent narrative of the client.

## Integrating Contradictory Sources of Information

The easiest and most straightforward sets of information are those that are consistent in that they support one another. These cases are the ones typically used for most teaching purposes and are nicely written up as textbook examples. For example, a child might be evaluated due to problems with academic performance. Behavioral observations indicate that he had a difficult time focusing on the testing tasks and was constantly moving around in his chair. In addition, rating scales from parents and teachers indicated poor attention, and his scores on the WISC-IV Working Memory Index were low. All these sources of information are consistent in suggesting that the child has problems with attention and hyperactivity. This also suggests a diagnosis of attention-deficit/hyperactivity disorder (ADHD). Wording on the report may emphasize this by stating something like "All sources of information supported the conclusion that. . . ."

In contrast, many assessments are not so straightforward and present report writers with challenges in coming to final conclusions. This typically occurs when there are disparities and inconsistencies in the information. The categories listed in Rapid Reference 3.1 and described below are possible reasons for explaining inconsistent assessment information.

---

RAPID REFERENCE 3.1: REASONS FOR INCONSISTENT ASSESSMENT INFORMATION

- Differences between the client's world and the assessment setting
- Differences among assessment instruments
- Nonrepresentative state of the client
- Client deception
- Cultural/ethnic considerations
- Self versus observer ratings
- Outlier scores

---

- *Differences between the client's world and assessment setting.* Sometimes seeming contradictions in assessment results may be due to the different demands of the environments where the data have been collected. In many ways, formal assessment is not representative of the client's everyday world in that the assessor structures the activities and usually minimizes distractions. For example, the child with academic difficulties discussed in the preceding paragraph may have had behavioral observations and ratings consistent with attentional difficulties, but a disparity might be noted in that the WISC-IV Working Memory Index score was in the average or even well-above-average range. This confusion is perhaps highlighted in that this index was even referred to at one time as "Freedom From Distractibility." This disparity may be resolved by noting that often persons with real-world attentional problems can do quite well on the Working Memory Index and other similar tasks because, during the assessment process, they do not have multiple distractions competing for their attention. Another example might be a patient with an acquired brain impairment who has done quite well on the WAIS-IV and Wechsler Memory Scale–IV (WMS-IV) but is reported to have considerable problems functioning at home and work. The reason for this may be that the client's problems may be primarily due to poor executive abilities. In other words, he has impairments in effectively planning, initiating, monitoring, and flexibly altering his behavior. Again, the structured testing situation does much of the planning and initiating behavior for the patient such that it might obscure problems with executive functioning. The seeming disparity in results may be resolved through a combination of careful interviewing with informants combined with administering specialized instruments sensitive to problems with executive functioning.

- *Differences in assessment instruments.* Another possible means of understanding seemingly contradictory test results are differences in how the assessment instruments obtain information and what they measure. For example, a client may not have elevated scores on MMPI-2 measures of disordered thinking, but there are indicators of a thought disorder that appear on the Rorschach. This may be due to the MMPI-2's being a self-report instrument in which the client states his impressions of how he thinks he is functioning. In contrast, the Rorschach is a performance-based personality measure that evaluates how the client actually responds to stimuli (Acklin, McDowell, Verschell, & Chan, 2000; Ganellen, 2007).

In other words, the MMPI-2 measures explicit functioning, whereas the Rorschach is a measure of the client's more implicit processes. When confronted with the ambiguous, implicit, performance-based Rorschach inkblots, the client's thought processes might have become confused and disorganized in a way that may not have occurred with the more structured true–false questions on the MMPI-2. Thus, a resolution to the seemingly contradictory test scores is that the client may have a subtle, hidden, evolving thought disorder that he may not be fully aware of. Another example might be someone who rapidly responds in conversation but her WAIS-IV Processing Speed Index is quite low. At first this may not make sense. However, a careful consideration of the subtests on the Processing Speed Index indicates that they are all visual nonverbal tasks. In contrast, conversation/interviewing is a verbal auditory task. A reasonable hypothesis is that the client is slow for visual nonverbal tasks but, in contrast, is quite fast when responding to verbal auditory tasks such as a conversation or listening to instructions.

- *Nonrepresentative state of the client.* Sometimes clients might appear for assessment in a condition that does not represent their usual status with the result that test results may not be particularly representative of their typical level of functioning. This may include the client's being tired, having recently taken recreational substances, having a cold, or being in a state of acute crisis. This would most likely result in contradictions among various sources of assessment information. For example, cognitive tests might have been given to a client during an initial session. If the same client were again given cognitive tests several days later but had a cold, it is quite likely that he or she would have performed relatively poorly on selected subtests for the second session. Assuming that the clinician still wanted to include the data from the second session, he or she would need to make the interpretations cautiously, perhaps stating something like "Since the client had a cold during the second session, the results are likely to represent a slight underestimate of his cognitive abilities. . . ."

- *Client deception.* There are a number of situations where a client might purposely present him- or herself in an overly favorable or overly negative manner. Overly positive results may be given by a person applying for a job or from a parent being evaluated to help decide child custody. The parent who is seeking custody of his child may appear quite well adjusted on the Personality Assessment Inventory (PAI), but, in contrast, a record review indicates domestic violence and substance abuse. In contrast, overly negative test results may come from plaintiffs seeking compensation during litigation or a defendant who is trying to plead not guilty by reason of insanity. Making a final determination of deception needs to be made with caution as the consequences can have a major effect on the person. As a rule of thumb, three different instruments/ tests strategies should be used to determine the possibility of faking bad. There should ideally be consistency among each of these sources. In addition, report writers should be cautious with their phrasing. Rather than stridently stating that the client was "malingering" or "faking bad," more appropriate phrases might be that he had "inconsistent effort" or "the results are consistent, although not necessarily definitive, with the defendant's exaggerating his personal difficulties." In contrast, terms such as *faking, lying, deception*, and *malingering* should generally be avoided.

- *Cultural/ethnic considerations.* Another possible reason for seemingly contradictory assessment information might be culturally unique responses by the test taker. Thus, a client might have a history in which she was functioning quite well but some of her test scores might be surprisingly low. This would be particularly true if the client was tested in a language that was not her first language or if she had limited knowledge of the culture or values that the test was based on. In cases where clients used a language that was not their first language, it would be expected that their verbally based scores on ability tests would be relatively lower and be an underestimate of their optimal level of functioning. This interpretation should then be stated by the report writer. However, sometimes values may also make a difference in test performance. For example, a client from a culture that had a minimum sense of time urgency may do relatively poorly on speeded tests of ability. Again, report writers should include this qualification to any interpretations related to speed of processing. This might include a statement such as "The client scored quite low in tests that required him to respond rapidly, which is likely to reflect the influence of the culture he grew up in, which does not emphasize a strong sense of time urgency."

- *Self versus observer ratings.* Sometimes confusing results can occur when the client makes self-ratings, and then ratings by another person are made that seem to contradict the client's self-ratings (Acklin et al., 2000; Ganellen, 2007). Whereas there is generally good agreement between self versus other observations of *external* behavior, disparities are common for more *internal* forms of behavior. Thus, a child might report inner feelings of hopelessness and despair, whereas a parent may be unaware of these feelings. This may be in part due to the more hidden nature of the feelings. It may also suggest that the parent is not particularly attuned to or accepting of difficult feelings the child may have. This would explain the disparity but also highlight an additional and potentially important family dynamic to evaluate.

- *Outlier scores.* When a large amount of information is collected, there are sometimes high or low scores that can be discarded because they are meaningless. In other words, they just don't make sense given the totality of what is known about the client, despite efforts on the part of the clinician to interpret why the unusual score has occurred. Perhaps the client lost his focus, did not understand the instructions, or became temporarily fatigued. Sometimes asking the client what happened on the scale/subtest in question can be quite useful. The challenge to the clinician is to discard the score only when he or she is reasonably certain that it does not reveal something particularly unique and important about the person being evaluated.

Ideally, clinicians will resolve assessment contradictions in a way that will not only make sense but will also deepen and expand the meaning of the assessment. Thus, working through the possible categories of disparate results presents a challenge that is potentially filled with opportunity. Coming to the optimal conclusions involves good reasoning based on knowledge of clinical conditions, research, and clinical experience. Hopefully, a consideration of these categories will improve how clinicians work to understand the meaning of the assessment results. Despite such efforts, it is sometimes necessary for the report writer to simply state that she can't make definitive conclusions. She might then offer interpretations that are speculative and admit to how tentative these interpretations are. In cases of deception, a report writer might find it useful to describe how a client has presented him- or herself but then elaborate on why this isn't a valid description. A slightly different strategy might be to simply state that the results are confusing and to state why. This may result in further exploration by readers of the report that might lead to a later but more accurate understanding of the client. In these cases, clinicians might need to first challenge their need to be more definitive.

## Types of Subheadings

As noted previously, the Impressions and Interpretations section should ideally be divided into domains of functioning. However, PRWA users can also customize any aspects of the report including the subheadings according to their needs. Some of the most common functional domains are cognitive, personality, interpersonal, coping style, and client strengths. A client's *cognitive abilities* are often described first since their level of cognitive functioning provides a framework or foundation for understanding the rest of the person. It may include a quite wide range of abilities. If organized around the WAIS-IV/WISC-IV, cognitive abilities can be grouped according to the subheadings of general ability, verbal abilities, perceptual reasoning, working memory, and speed of processing. Other abilities might be memory, executive functioning, emotional intelligence, and level of sensory–motor functioning. Cognitive assessment within psychiatric contexts might include the degree to which the patient's thinking is organized, abstract versus concrete, level of awareness, or whether there are any bizarre associations or unusual tangents.

Most reports organize cognitive results according to a broad test of intellectual functioning such as the WAIS-IV or WISC-IV. It is traditional to include the IQ/index classification, scaled score, and percentile. Thus, a typical sentence might read something like "Mr. Smith's overall ability was in the Superior Range (WAIS-IV = 130) or the 98th percentile when compared to his age-related peers." In order to place this into more everyday language a report writer might also wish to add something like "This means that only 2% of the population would have scored this high." Some report writers also recommend including confidence intervals (i.e., "There is a 95% chance that the scores would fall between 125 and 133"). In some cases this might be useful or even required. However, the approach of integrative assessment is to minimize technical information like confidence intervals in favor of clarity and making the report reader friendly. This orientation is consistent with research on psychological reports that indicate consumers have often rated them as overly technical and test oriented (see Groth-Marnat & Horvath, 2006; Harvey, 2006). This is also consistent with the finding that most clinicians avoid including test scores such as IQ/Index results since they are concerned that the information might be misinterpreted (Pieniadz & Kelland, 2001).

*Personality* refers to a person's unique and enduring characteristics that influence his or her thoughts, behaviors, and motivations. A greater understanding of symptoms can often be made based on personality. If, for example, a person experiencing depression has a narcissistic style to his personality, it is likely that the depression is closely related to some sort of rupture to his narcissistic beliefs. In contrast, a dependent personality style would suggest that depression occurs largely due to a real or imagined threat to a person in the client's life who organizes and takes responsibility for the client. Thus, a description of a symptom might provide information on how the symptom is expressed, but an understanding of the underlying personality tells the clinician how the client got to the place of having the symptom as well as the underlying dynamics that keep the symptom going. Knowledge of personality can also be used to tailor psychotherapeutic intervention to optimize outcome (Harwood, Beutler, & Groth-Marnat, 2011).

The personality section of a report usually lists and expands on the main features of personality. Thus, a person high on extroversion would be likely to cope by spending time around people, would do well in occupations that require extensive interaction, and would be likely to have a large circle of friends. Other personality features might include openness to experience, how conscientious he is, the degree to which he focuses on physiological complaints, and his level of assertiveness. Different tests will provide different types of information. For example, the MMPI-2 will provide descriptions of personality relevant to psychopathology and coping. In contrast, the NEO Personality Inventory–3

(NEO-PI-3) or the Myers-Briggs Type Indicator (MBTI) will provide aspects of personality that reflect normal types of functioning. This is illustrated in that the conceptualizations of introversion underlying the MBTI and the MMPI-2 are quite different. This should be reflected in how interpretations of introversion derived from these two tests are made.

One of the essential features of personality assessment is to understand the person's *core conflicts*. Usually, these revolve around dependency, hostility, and sexuality. This means it would often be important to discuss how the person copes with these areas. For example, strong overt behaviors of independence may mask an underlying sense of dependence the person is not comfortable with. In contrast, another person may have a quite secure sense of the interplay of independence and dependence in their relationships. Hostility is an additional crucial area. How does the client express hostility? Is it direct and expressed in a destructive manner? Or has the client learned to express it in a manner that is engaged and ends up being constructive. Or perhaps she is quite uncomfortable with her anger and has learned to express it in a more indirect, passive-aggressive manner. As noted previously, sexuality is something that many interviewers do not evaluate. This is unfortunate in that much of a person's sense of identity is related to how he or she views and acts on his or her sexuality. How strong is his or her need for sex, and how does this impact his or her relationships? Is his or her sexuality used as a means of gaining self-affirmation? Or perhaps sex and his or her sense of sexuality has caused the client pain such that it has no longer become a part of how he or she acts. What might be the dynamics behind any unusual sexual practices?

Understanding the clients' roles and *patterns in relationships* is also often important to include in a psychological report. A useful conceptualization is the extent the client's relationships are centered on the continuum of love versus hostility and dominance versus submission. This will inform the reader on the extent the client is warm/cold, how disclosing he might be, and how much he seeks to control others. Is he direct or more indirect in his interactions? What is the extent to which he is comfortable with conflict as opposed to wanting to avoid it at all costs? When conflicts do occur, how does he typically try to work through them? Is he passive, assertive, or hostile? Is he psychologically minded, or does he spend little time reflecting on himself and others?

How the client *copes with stress* is important for most types of assessments. One continuum is to consider the extent the client has an externalizing versus an internalizing style. Externalizers are likely to consider factors outside themselves as being the cause of their problems. As a result, they are more likely to blame others and externalize their behavior in the form of becoming angry, creating conflict, using substances, or other forms of acting out. They justify these behaviors as being caused by what others have done. In contrast, internalizers are more likely to consider the cause of their difficulties as being due to factors within themselves. As a result, they will be more likely to reflect on their part in any conflicts and take personal responsibility, with the result that they will be more likely to become depressed or anxious. Sometimes a person will not have a clearly defined style and will use a combination of externalizing and internalizing. Understanding this basic dimension has strong implications for the type of psychotherapy the person will benefit from (Beutler, Harwood, Kimpara, Verdirame, & Blau, 2011; Harwood et al., 2011). Externalizers will be more likely to respond well to behavioral, symptom-oriented interventions that focus on building specific skills. In contrast, internalizers tend to respond to psychotherapy that emphasizes insight and emotional awareness. The MMPI-2 can also be seen as a model for understanding coping with each of the clinical scales representing somewhat different strategies. For example, clients scoring high on scale 1 (hypochnodriasis) will be likely to place a greater focus on problems with bodily functioning when under stress. In contrast, clients with high scores on scale 9 (mania) will speed up their level of activity. Both of these strategies will serve the purpose of distracting them from underlying painful feelings. Finally, it is often useful to ask clients what they themselves do to better deal with stress. This will result in a wide variety of activities such as talking with friends, exercising, being in nature, eating, shopping, drinking, meditating, praying, or taking medication.

Many reports, especially those developed within educational, organizational, or rehabilitation contexts, need to elaborate on a client's *career* options. Personality has clear implications such as tailoring vocational pursuits toward the extent the client prefers to be around people (extroversion–introversion). In addition, a person's cognitive abilities can be tailored around his or her cognitive strengths and weaknesses. For example, a person with high nonverbal abilities would be likely to do well in careers in auto repair, architecture, or interior design. The final major link in career assessment is matching the client's interests with possible careers (Lowman, 1991).

Rehabilitation, psychiatric, and psychoeducational settings often need to understand clients' ability to function in their everyday world (*activities of daily living*). This is particularly the case when case management decisions need to be made regarding the extent a client can function independently. For example, a complete assessment of intellectual disabilities (mental retardation) needs to include not only the formal level of intelligence, but the degree to which clients can function on their own. Similarly, many clients in medical/rehabilitation settings need to have complete assessments of their activities of daily living. This may include evaluating such areas as managing money, social adjustment, managing home and transportation, health and safety, and ability to shop. Level of assistance may range from being able to function independently to needing 24/7 hands-on care. Specialized instruments include the Vineland Adaptive Behavior Scales–II (Sparrow, Cichetti, & Balla, 2005) and the Independent Living Scales (Loeb, 1996). Occupational therapists have a large number of instruments to assess activities of daily living as well as numerous strategies for assisting patients. This means that if problems with activities of daily living are encountered, further assessment and intervention by an occupational therapist may be an important recommendation.

Since much of the information in a psychological report relates to client difficulties, it is important to include a subsection on *client strengths* (see Snyder, Ritschel, Rand, & Berg, 2006). This creates balance, hope, and a more complete description, and can potentially lead to greater rapport with the client (Snyder, Lopez, & Pedrotti, 2011). A carefully worded listing of strengths also has the potential to facilitate client growth (Finn, 2012; Finn, Fischer, & Handler, 2012; Levak, Siegel, Nichols, & Stolberg, 2011). This information can potentially be used by therapists to create change by expanding on these strengths (Snyder et al., 2011).

Referral sources will often want report writers to make predictions for such things as response to treatment, recidivism, suicide risk, dangerousness, or success in a training program. Traditional psychological tests will rarely be useful in and of themselves. However, the data from the tests may be combined with other information to generate useful predictions. For example, the California Psychological Inventory has a number of formulas to help predict things such as college grade point average and success in medical school, police training programs, or parole (see Groth-Marnat, 2009a, pp. 373–383). Suicide risk assessment is a frequent referral question. Even if it is not part of the formal referral question, report writers should usually make a statement of suicide risk whenever a client reports being depressed. The most useful information is to consider whether there have been previous attempts, substance abuse, social supports, presence of a plan, lethality of the plan, and available resources to follow through on the plan. Information relevant to formal tests might be the clients' impulsivity and hopelessness. What would be ideal is to have a single resource available for clinicians that would describe and evaluate the common methods of making predictions (see Groth-Marnat, 2009b). However, even the best predictive strategies will still be subject to error. Long-term predictions are especially subject to a high degree of error.

Patient diagnosis is sometimes included in the Impressions and Interpretations section but at other times it has its own section or is part of the summary and recommendations. Diagnoses have the potential to guide treatment, develop greater understanding regarding the client, and provide access to resources. However, care needs to be taken as to whether a diagnosis is actually needed or even advisable. The short- and long-term impact of a diagnosis should also be given careful consideration. Some report writers might feel that diagnoses are overly reductionistic, become self-fulfilling, reduce options for patients, and allow clients to avoid responsibility for their behavior. Particular care needs to be taken with diagnosing personality disorders since the level of agreement among clinicians is low to nonexistent. A number of authors have even questioned whether or not many psychiatric diagnoses are scientifically valid terms and have further questioned whether they help improve treatment (Beutler & Malik, 2002; Groth-Marnat, Roberts, & Beutler, 2001; Houts, 2002). In order to increase the accuracy of diagnosis, clinicians will need to draw from all sources of assessment information and carefully make sure that this information matches the diagnostic criteria listed in the *DSM-5* (or International Classification of Diseases, 10th Revision [ICD-10]). Case concepualization might also include the primary, predisposing, and precipitating causes as well as include a biopsychosocial perspective. The following are useful terms report writers can use to designate the stage or degree of certainty they feel regarding the diagnoses: initial, deferred, principal, additional/comorbid, rule out (RO), admitting, tentative, working, final, discharge, in remission, or quiescent (Zuckerman, 2005).

## SUMMARY

The Summary section reviews the essential findings, answers each of the referral questions, and, based on this information, provides suggestions that can help solve the problem the referral source is confronted with. It integrates the history, observations, test results, records, and informant data to provide a synopsis of the client's level of functioning. Thus, it is the heart of the assessment process. In some cases, such as in many medical settings, it can be the only part of the report that is likely to be read. Therefore, it needs to be able to potentially stand on its own. It should be noted that sometimes the recommendations are listed in the heading along with the summary, and at other times they are given their own separate section. A separate Recommendations section is most likely to occur when the recommendations provided are complex and long.

The summary paragraph should begin with a brief restatement of the client and why he or she was referred ("Mr. Jones is a 48-year-old, European American, divorced male with 14 years of education, who presents with problems related to anxiety and depression."). This should then be followed by three to five sentences describing the strongest and most relevant findings. Often, this will summarize the cognitive results followed by essential information related to personality. The remaining one to three sentences vary depending on the type of report. Vocational reports might include information on interests or problem-solving style, whereas a personality/psychiatric report might list information related to diagnosis and might possibly include client strengths.

All reports should make sure that each of the referral questions has been concisely but completely answered. The suggested means of doing this is to number each one of the referral questions in the Referral Question section. This can be followed in the Summary and Recommendations by using the same numbers, briefly restating each question, and then providing a one- to four-sentence narrative that answers the question (see core strategy 1 in Chapter 2). In some cases it may not be possible to answer one or more of the referral questions, in which case this should be clearly stated

("... it is not possible to precisely determine the proportion that Mr. Client's stroke, traumatic brain injury, and chronic alcohol use account for the offenses he has been charged with committing"). Forensic reports typically have a section or subsection referred to as "Legal Issues" in which report writers answer the referral questions by providing their opinions related to the purpose of the evaluation.

## RECOMMENDATIONS

Recommendations are often considered to be the most important part of a report. In addition, developing recommendations relates to larger aspects of clinical practice. As a result, the next chapter (Chapter 4) is devoted exclusively to this topic. However, some initial general guidelines are summarized later. Recommendations should include a series of practical, specific, achievable things that the referral source and/or the client can do to help with the issues that have been presented. Reports tend to be considered most helpful if the recommendations are specific rather than general (Armengol, 2001; Finn, Moes, & Kaplan, 2001). Thus, a recommendation that simply states the client should be referred "for rehabilitation" is less informative than stating that the client should begin "rehabilitation at the Metropolis Rehabilitation Institute focusing on a multidisciplinary approach that would emphasize cognitive retraining, speech therapy, mindfulness-based stress reduction, vocational counseling, and occupational therapy."

Sometimes report writers should be cautious in making recommendations since they may be sending the report to a setting in which the referral source feels that a team should be making the recommendations rather than the report writer. In other cases, the referral source may not actually want recommendations to be made since the referring agency may then be legally bound to follow through on each of the recommendations. Many, if not most, forensic reports do not need to include recommendations. Report writers also need to be cautious that they do not extend beyond their professional boundaries or level of competence. This may occur when the professional psychologist makes specific medication recommendations for a report written to a psychiatrist or suggests that a neurologist do an MRI (magnetic resonance imaging).

One useful strategy is to prioritize the recommendations so that the most important ones come first. For example, intervention for a patient who represents a danger to self or others should be given precedence over other types of recommendations. Another useful guideline that will be expanded in the next chapter is to provide the rationale for the recommendation followed by the recommendation itself ("In order to reduce Jimmy's attentional difficulties he should be referred for a medical evaluation to . . .").

The PRWA allows report writers to select from a large menu of different recommendations (see also Chapter 4). Each of the different types of reports has a large number of recommendations organized and tailored toward the type of report that is being written. For example, a career-oriented report might recommend such things as interviewing or "shadowing" someone already working in the career of interest. In contrast, a neuropsychological report might recommend speech therapy or further evaluation by an occupational therapist. Since there will be so many possible recommendations in the software menu, it may mean that report writers could be tempted to provide too many recommendations. However, restraint is urged, and only those recommendations that are most relevant, acceptable to the client, and are available in the community should be included.

## SIGNATURE/TITLE

The Signature/Title is where report writers sign their report along with including their title and date. The importance of this section is that it means that the professional psychologist is assuring the reader that she is personally responsible for the contents of the report.

## APPENDIX

The Appendix is an optional section that typically includes actual test scores (see Test Results section). As noted previously, the PRWA includes a menu that provides summary tables and graphs that report writers can use to portray the client's test scores. An Appendix section might also include duplicates of client attempts to reproduce designs, clock drawings, human figure drawings, or important examples of TAT stories. Additional information might include computer interpretive narratives or copies of medical, academic, work, or military records.

# Recommended Reading

Braaten, E. B. (2007). *The child clinician's report writing handbook*. New York, NY: Guilford Press.

Levak, R. W., & Hogan, S. (2011). Integrating and applying assessment information: Decision making, patient feedback, and consultation. In T. M. Harwood, L. E. Beutler, & G. Groth-Marnat (Eds.), *Integrative assessment of adult personality* (3rd ed., pp. 373–409). New York, NY: Guilford Press.

O'Hanlon, B., & Bertolino, B. (2012). *The therapist's notebook on positive psychology: Activities, exercises, and handouts*. New York, NY: Routledge.

Scherer, M. (2011). Assistive technologies and other supports for people with brain impairment. New York, NY: Springer.

Sommers-Flanagan, R., & Sommers-Flanagan, J. (2009). *Clinical interviewing* (4th ed.). Hoboken, NJ: Wiley.

Zuckerman, E. L. (2005). *The clinician's thesaurus three: A guidebook for wording psychological reports* (6th ed.). New York, NY: Guilford Press.

# CHAPTER 4

# Recommendations

Recommendations can be considered the capstone of a report. These provide a transition from the assessment results and into how the information can be used to make decisions regarding a client. Thus, the assessment results themselves provide the scaffolding that will provide support for the recommendations. This chapter provides a means of understanding how recommendations can be tailored to the client and how they are organized in the Psychological Report Writing Assistant (PRWA), as well as a guide to resources available to assist with treatment planning.

The PRWA provides users with a variety of categories and types of recommendations. Once users of the software click on to the recommendations section of the composition window, an icon will appear in the ribbon bar between the composition pane (top right) and the example report narratives (bottom left; see Chapter 6). When they click onto the recommendation icon, users will then note that the category of recommendation they are interested in (e.g., treatment, self-help) will appear to the left of the screen. Users can then fine-tune their selection of recommendations by locating various subcategories they might be interested in (e.g., modes of psychotherapy, medication). Once they click on to the subcategory, a specific recommendation will appear (e.g., individual psychotherapy, family psychotherapy). For example, the treatment recommendations in the psychoeducational report module include a subcategory for educational interventions, and these are even further divided into accommodations for reading, writing, math, attention, and testing. Report writers can easily click the box to the left of a recommendation they would like to include and it will automatically be inserted into the report.

An important caution is that, given the large number of possible recommendations, it may be tempting to insert too many recommendations into the report. The result may be that readers of the report may have a difficult time deciding which, if any, recommendations should be followed. As a general rule, somewhere between four and six recommendations should be selected. Another issue is that most of the recommendations provided in the software program are not, and cannot be, tailored to the specifics of the client. As a result, attention needs to be given to how report writers can edit the recommendations they have selected from the PRWA so that they will be tailored to the individual aspects of the person.

## TAILORING RECOMMENDATIONS TO THE CLIENT

An essential strategy in writing recommendations is to "wrap" relevant recommendations in the rationale for why they are being suggested. This can serve to provide a link between the presenting problem, findings of the assessment, and possible solutions. For example, a report writer might potentially list a recommendation as simply being for "cognitive behavior therapy." In contrast, he or she might individualize the recommendation more by writing something like "In order to reduce Mary's anxiety, it is recommended that she attend 12 sessions of cognitive behavior therapy." Additional examples of phrases that can be used to introduce and provide the rationale for recommendations are provided in Rapid Reference 4.1. The PRWA sometimes includes these phrases in its menu of recommendations, but most of the time it does not. When it is not present, report writers need to evaluate whether it would be useful to use the previously suggested strategy.

One of the primary tasks of a report writer is to accumulate sufficient knowledge and resources to provide useful recommendations. Often, practicing clinicians develop their own lists that continue to grow as they gain more experience in the context and community they are working in. These include both general recommendations (e.g., "individual psychotherapy") as well as ones more specific to their community (e.g., ". . . assessment at Metroville Sleep Disorders clinic by Dr. Smith at 111

RAPID REFERENCE 4.1: SAMPLE INTRODUCTORY
RATIONALES FOR RECOMMENDATIONS

- Due to John's difficulties with attention . . .
- As a result of Mary's visuospatial difficulties, it is recommended that . . .
- In order to reduce Ms. Cognitive's level of anxiety, it is recommended that . . .
- Given George's potential for self-harm it is recommended that . . .

Treeborn Lane, Metroville, CA"). One useful resource is for clinicians to refer to the Wiley Practice planners that help practitioners develop treatment plans for a variety of client populations and contexts including adults, children, college students, older adults, and clients in rehabilitation and medical settings (e.g., Jongsma & Peterson, 2006; Jongsma, Peterson, & McInnis, 2006).

Framing recommendations within the context of culture can often be crucial. Due to increased globalization and extensive migration, most countries have sizable subgroups from different cultures. For example, a third of the United States is composed of diverse cultural groups, and fully 75% of Hawaii and 57% of California are composed of ethnic minorities (United States Census Bureau, 2007). In addition, 20% of the U.S. population speaks a language other than English in their home (Shin & Kominski, 2010). This means that psychologists doing assessment will need to be aware of the various needs these groups might have. This is also consistent with the mandate by the American Psychological Association that professional practice be guided by knowledge, awareness, and sensitivity toward cultural differences.

The challenge for report writers is to phrase recommendations in such a way as to take into account cultural perspectives (see Smith, Rodriguez, & Bernal, 2011). For example, persons from diverse cultural backgrounds, and particularly Asian Americans, may need greater preparation for counseling than majority groups. Thus, a recommendation might state that it would be crucial for the client to be clearly informed of the nature of therapy, the role of the therapist and client, typical problems that may be encountered, the difference between a physician and a counselor, and to clarify any misconceptions that the client might have. Assessment may also involve a culturally oriented understanding of the client's explanation as to why they have the problems that they are experiencing and what they think can be done to correct them. Thus, recommendations may need to take these into account (e.g., "Given the client's belief in a spiritual understanding of their current difficulties, the treating therapist may wish to consult and collaborate with an indigenous healer to optimize treatment outcome."). One frequent source of conflict and resulting dysfunction is when children acculturate more rapidly than their immigrant parents. The parents may react by trying to regain what they perceive as lost status by becoming more rigid and authoritarian. This can result in exacerbating the problem. Thus, a recommendation might focus on having a therapist understand, describe, and mediate this source of conflict. The preceding examples highlight the finding that adapting recommendations and treatment to a client's cultural background has been associated with greater benefit from interventions (Smith et al., 2011).

One major challenge in providing recommendations is to increase the likelihood that they will be followed (see Geffken, Keeley, Kellison, Storch, & Rodrigue, 2006). The efficacy of assessment itself can often be gauged by the extent to which the decisions or interventions based on assessment are actually carried out. The following strategies can be used to increase the adherence to recommendations:

- Avoid overwhelming the report consumer with too many recommendations.
- Be specific (e.g., include provider name, contact details, length of treatment, cost).
- Understand the relevance of treatment from the perspective of the client.
- Consider family, community, financial, cultural, and other contextual factors that will impact adherence to recommendations.
- Connect each recommendation with what symptom the recommendation might help (e.g., "In order to reduce Mr. Client's depression, 10 sessions of . . .").
- Help the client integrate the results of the assessment and understand how the recommendations might be of help.

- Enhance motivation to change (e.g., motivational interviewing, use Participation Enhancement Intervention [Nock & Kazdin, 2005]).
- Set up any appointments in collaboration with the client and when he or she is present.

As noted above, it is generally useful to provide recommendations that are specific. This can refer both to whom and where the treatment will be provided, as well as what these recommendations actually entail. Sometimes it can be useful to attach information on a clinic or type of treatment as an appendix to the report. Having said this, it is not always wise to be specific since, in some instances, the report writer may not have sufficient knowledge related to a problem and treatment for the problems to be specific. For example, a professional psychologist rarely knows the types of interventions a speech pathologist or special education teacher might wish to use. In these cases its best to instead give a general recommendation and add that another professional should develop a more detailed treatment plan (e.g., ". . . refer for evaluation and treatment planning by a speech pathologist"). Thus, report writers should consistently question whether or not they are providing recommendations within their area of competency.

## CATEGORIES OF RECOMMENDATIONS

The PRWA divides recommendations into the following categories: treatment, education/self-help, placement, further evaluation, alteration in environment, and miscellaneous (see Table 4.1). These should provide a comprehensive array of options. There are also other possible ways of organizing recommendations that can vary according to the setting and needs of the client. One strategy is a hierarchical organization beginning with levels of intervention and extending to modality and ending with the specific skills that need to be learned within the modality. The *levels* of intervention relate to setting and degree of restrictiveness. These may include placement in the home, foster care, outpatient treatment, partial hospitalization, or inpatient treatment. Deciding on the proper level is a crucial issue when the patient is a danger to self or others. The *modality* of intervention refers to the general model of intervention and may include such options as cognitive behavior therapy, insight-oriented therapy,

| TABLE 4.1 | CATEGORIES AND EXAMPLES OF TREATMENT RECOMMENDATIONS |
|---|---|

| Category | Examples |
|---|---|
| Treatment | Psychotherapy, special education, speech therapy, occupational therapy, medication, meditation, mediation |
| Education/Self-help | Self-help books, films, web sites, support groups; computer-aided interventions |
| Placement | Group home, nursing home, 24/7 observation, joint custody, inpatient care |
| Further evaluation | Reevaluation with selected portions of current tests, medication review, medical exam |
| Alter environment | Medication alarm, internal/external reminders |
| Miscellaneous | Revoke driver's license, wear MedicAlert bracelet, probation, homework (gratitude letter, practice self-statements) |

Adapted from Groth-Marnat (2009a).

Dialectical Behavior Therapy, anger management, or family therapy. Finally, *skills* refer to which behaviors, attitudes, or emotions the client needs to change. These may include developing greater emotional balance, reduced expressions of anger, better sleep hygiene, good nutrition, or more exercise.

## Treatment

The greatest focus of most reports is to provide suggestions for treatment. This can include a wide variety of areas such as models of psychotherapy, medication, rehabilitation, improving sleep, parenting skills, interventions for suicide, interventions for specific types of diagnoses, areas for client exploration, accommodations to the client's disability, and referral for treatment by appropriate professionals. The PRWA includes each of these categories, which are then divided into separate subcategories with specific recommendations for each one. For example, models of psychotherapy might list cognitive behavior therapy, psychodynamic therapy, systematic desensitization, or Dialectical Behavior Therapy. Selecting one of these and leaving it identical to the wording in the software would rarely be sufficient. It is instead up to the author to edit them so that they would apply to the person being assessed. For example, rather than stating "psychodynamic therapy" an author might state something like "Given Mr. Smith's internalizing coping style combined with his repetitive patterns of problematic interpersonal relationships, he would most likely benefit from psychodynamically oriented psychotherapy." Another example related to potential problems with driving might be the following: "Given the patient's current visuospatial difficulties, attentional problems, reduced processing speed, and decreased insight related to safety awareness, it is recommended that Ms. Smith not operate a motor vehicle. She should be reevaluated before making the decision to drive again and will likely need to attend a driver's safety program and receive on-the-road evaluation."

**Treatment Planning for Psychotherapy**    Most psychological reports include recommendations for psychotherapy. These vary widely based on the report writer's training, experience, knowledge of the research, understanding of client needs, and personal views on what results in client change. The three general approaches are to tailor treatment recommendations based on matching the intervention with diagnosis ("differential therapeutics"), focusing on common characteristics, and tailoring interventions based on relevant client characteristics (see Groth-Marnat, 2009a; Groth-Marnat, Roberts, & Beutler, 2001). Each of the three approaches has different strategies for how recommendations will be constructed. *Matching treatment with diagnosis* is both time-honored and is deeply entrenched in current models of health care. It follows the approach used in medicine where it is usually crucial to develop an accurate diagnosis and then use the treatment having the strongest base of evidence to optimize the outcome. If a patient has a bacterial infection, then it clearly makes sense to identify the type of bacteria and then use antibiotics that have been found to be effective in treating that type of infection. This same model has pervaded much of treatment planning in psychology. Thus, many manuals on treatment planning emphasize matching treatment with diagnoses such as recommending exposure and response (ritual) prevention for treating obsessive–compulsive disorder, interpersonal therapy for depression, or psychodynamic therapy for personality disorders. Usually, insurance reimbursement is dependent on making diagnoses and developing a treatment plan based on the diagnosis the client has been given.

In some cases, making an accurate diagnosis is both crucial and is essential in designing an effective intervention. For example, children diagnosed with a bipolar disorder would be likely to require mood-stabilizing medication. A misdiagnosis of attention-deficit/hyperactivity disorder (ADHD) with a resulting administration of amphetamines can potentially have negative consequences. A wide variety of treatments have been used to successfully treat such problems as depressive and anxiety disorders (APA Task Force on Evidence-Based Practice, 2006; Barlow, 2004, 2008; Shedler, 2010; Sturmey & Hersen, 2012). An important caution with matching treatment according to diagnosis is that it has often been found that quite a large number of treatments are effective in treating the same disorder with very little difference in patient outcome (Beutler, 2009; Nathan & Gorman, 2007; Shedler, 2010).

Despite the success of matching treatment according to diagnosis, *common factors* have been found to be of equal or greater importance in understanding outcome (Norcross, 2011; Norcross & Lambert, 2011; Wampold, 2001, 2010). The primary common factor is understanding and enhancing the quality of the therapeutic relationship. While this is a general principle, the specifics are in conceptualizing what factors are likely to enhance as opposed to rupture the quality of the relationship. Often, assessment can help identify these factors. For example, there are predictable challenges that are likely to occur when working with a person with narcissistic tendencies. Initially, the client is likely to compliment the therapist as a strategy to both control the relationship and increase the likelihood that the therapist will reciprocate by similarly enhancing the self-esteem of the client. At some point, the therapist will be likely to challenge the client, which will result in anger, retaliation, and possible termination of therapy. Somewhat different dynamics will form with clients who have depressive, dependent, borderline, or obsessive–compulsive styles. This means that an important contribution of the report writer would be to describe these predictable challenges so that the treating psychotherapist can prepare for these challenges and even collaborate with the client on how best to work with them. Thus, the recommendations coming from a common factors approach may be quite different from those emerging from matching treatments with diagnoses.

A third approach is *matching relevant client characteristics with treatment approaches*. For example, clients with high levels of hypnotizability do well when hypnosis is used, particularly if they are being treated for physiological conditions such as pain (Lynn & Shindler, 2002). It has also been found that clients who are resistant to treatment do best when the therapist approaches the client in either a collaborative, nondirective manner or when the therapist uses paradoxical strategies (Beutler, Harwood, Michelson, Song, & Holman, 2011; Beutler, Moleiro, & Talebi, 2002). Beutler and colleagues (Beutler, Clarkin, & Bongar, 2001; Harwood, Beutler, & Groth-Marnat, 2011) have reviewed over 100 possible client characteristic and found that there are seven qualities that have been found to be highly relevant for treatment planning. This approach thus addresses the question as to what type of person will respond best to which type of treatment. Research has indicated that clinicians who tailor their approach to clients based on an understanding of client characteristics will be able to improve their outcomes. This model has been found to account for more of the outcome variation than either the quality of the therapeutic relationship or tailoring treatment according to diagnosis (see Beutler, 2009; Groth-Marnat et al., 2001). When predictions are based on the quality of the relationship combined with relevant client characteristics, up to 90% of the outcome variance can be accounted for (Beutler, 2009). Report writers using this approach will provide recommendations primarily derived from matching treatment to relevant client characteristic. The next section provides greater detail into this approach.

**Systematic Treatment Selection/Innerlife Model** An overview of Systematic Treatment Selection (STS) is available in the treatment planning chapter in the *Handbook of Psychological Assessment* (5th ed.; Groth-Marnat, 2009a), *Integrative Assessment of Adult Personality* (3rd ed.; Harwood, Beutler, & Groth-Marnat, 2011) and especially through the innerlife.com consumer-oriented web site. The treatment-planning chapter (Chapter 14) of the *Handbook of Psychological Assessment* details how assessment information can be used to evaluate each of the seven client characteristics. Assessment can range from brief clinical judgment (". . . this client seems to be high in resistance based on interview observations and history") to formal psychological tests (". . . moderate scores on MMPI-2 scales 4 and 6 suggest a resistant interpersonal style"). The various client characteristics are evaluated in the innerlife.com program and then used to provide clients and other consumers with relevant treatment planning information. Specific areas that are addressed in innerlife.com to help clients taking the questionnaire include the following:

- What problems do I have, and which should be treated first?
- Am I at risk for suicidal, aggressive, or abusive behavior?
- What is the optimal treatment approach for each of my problem areas?
- I'm not a psychotherapist—what should the treatment approach "look like" when I meet with my therapist?
- How much time in treatment should I expect?
- What treatments should I avoid?
- How about self-help options?
- What's available for me and my particular challenges?
- What options are available if I do or do not have insurance to cover mental health treatment?

Although the answers to these question are directed toward the client, much of the information can be extracted, edited, and incorporated into a psychological report. For example, the question "What problems do *I* have, and which should be treated first?" becomes "What problems do *they* have, and which should be treated first?" and so forth.

Research on STS/Innerlife indicates that, if psychotherapy is to be optimized, the greatest payoff is to assess and take in to consideration the domains listed in Table 4.2 (see also Beutler, 2009; Groth-Marnat et al., 2001). A report Impressions and Interpretations section might even be formatted to include subheadings that would expand on these domains. More typically, they might be listed under a single heading such as "client characteristics for treatment planning" or merely be referred to in the Summary and/or Recommendations sections ("Ms. Smith's high level of resistance suggests that she would benefit from a collaborative, nondirective approach."). Table 4.2 also indicates the treatment implications given relevant client characteristics. For example, a client with an externalizing coping style would be most likely to benefit from a behavioral, symptom-oriented approach (and treatment efforts may even deteriorate if internal, insight-oriented approaches are used; Beutler, Harwood, Kimpara, Verdirame, & Blau, 2011).

| TABLE 4.2 | SYSTEMATIC TREATMENT SELECTION/INNERLIFE: CLIENT CHARACTERISTICS AND TREATMENT IMPLICATIONS |
|---|---|

| Client Characteristic | Treatment Consideration |
|---|---|
| Functional impairment | Restrictiveness (inpatient/outpatient) |
| | Intensity (duration and frequency) |
| | Medical vs. psychosocial interventions |
| | Prognosis |
| | Urgency of achieving goals |
| Social support | Cognitive behavioral vs. relationship enhancement |
| | Duration of treatment |
| | Psychosocial intervention vs. medication |
| | Possible group interventions |
| Problem complexity/chronicity | Narrow symptom-oriented vs. internal insight-oriented |
| Coping style (internal vs. external) | Behavioral symptom-oriented vs. internal insight-oriented interventions |
| Resistance | Supportive, nondirective, or paradoxical vs. structured, directive interventions |
| Subjective distress | Increase/decrease arousal |
| Stages of change | Exploration and awareness vs. overt behavioral or interpersonal change |

Adapted from Groth-Marnat (2009a).

The PRWA program includes an abbreviated version of Systematic Treatment Selection/Innerlife. The STS icon appears just to the right of the recommendations icon when users click onto the Recommendations section. Based on all sources of assessment information, the report writer is asked to rate the client on each of the seven client characteristics. This means that users should already be familiar with what these characteristics are and how to assess them (see details in the treatment planning chapter of the *Handbook of Psychological Assessment*, 5th ed.; Groth-Marnat, 2009a). Treatment recommendations emerge when the client is rated either high or low on one or more of the characteristics. For example, a high rating on the client's level of subjective (motivational) distress would result in a treatment recommendation that reads, "In order to reduce Ms. Jones' level of distress enough for her to be fully involved in therapy, she would need to benefit from one or more of the following techniques: progressive muscle relaxation, aerobic exercise, meditation, emotional 'venting,' reassurance, emotional support, time management, or thought stopping." In cases when all or most of the client characteristics are rated in the average range, few clear recommendations will emerge. In contrast, a series of high, or in some cases low, ratings would result in a number of clear, strong recommendations.

**Best Practices and Treatment Planning**   The American Psychological Association and the American Psychiatric Association have developed and are in the process of refining best practice guidelines. These have involved summarizing the findings of numerous studies to extract information relevant to helping practitioners decide how best to work with common clinical situations and different types of clients. Using these guidelines is intended to enhance treatment as well as reduce malpractice complaints. However, the guidelines are not intended to be absolute and overly restrictive. There should still be room for integrating the guidelines with clinicians' experience, expertise, and client preferences.

While some of the guidelines have been completed and are available to practitioners, others are still being developed. For example, the American Psychiatric Association web site (see below) currently has fully developed guidelines for problems such as acute stress/posttraumatic stress disorder, Alzheimer's disease, bipolar disorder, borderline personality disorder, eating disorders, obsessive–compulsive disorder, major depressive disorder, panic disorder, schizophrenia, substance use, and suicidal behavior. These are available in the form of downloadable brochures that range between 10 and 30 pages. A similar listing is available through the American Psychological Association's Division 12 (Society of Clinical Psychology). Their web site (see Rapid Reference 4.2) includes a wide range of disorders along with specific treatments, the degree of support for these treatments, research articles, and where training can be obtained for the various interventions. The American Psychological Association (APA) has also developed guidelines for general aspects of practice such as forensic psychology, record keeping, child custody evaluations, practice with older adults, sexual orientation, disabilities, dementia/cognitive decline, pharmacological involvement, and test user qualifications (see web site below and APA, 2012a, 2012b, 2012c). Report writers making treatment recommendations are advised to become familiar with these sources and integrate them into their reports (see also Sturmey & Hersen, 2012). A further valuable resource is the Oxford University Press series of short books on "treatments that work" that provides evidence-based guidelines for disorders such as chronic pain (Otis, 2007) obsessive–compulsive disorder (Foa, Yadin, & Lichner, 2012), insomnia (Edinger & Carney, 2008), and posttraumatic stress disorder (Foa, Hembree, & Rothbaum, 2007).

---

**RAPID REFERENCE 4.2: ORGANIZATIONS AND WEB SITES PROVIDING BEST PRACTICES GUIDELINES**

American Psychological Association: www.apa.org/practice/prof.html
American Psychiatric Association: www.psychiatryonline.com/pracGuide/
pracGuideTopic_9.aspx
PracticeWise Evidence-Based Services [PWEBS]: www.practicewise.com
Society of Clinical Psychology: www.psychologicaltreatments.org

---

## Education/Self-Help

Self-help resources include self-help books, autobiographies, films, self-help support groups, Internet materials, and computer-aided psychotherapy (see Marks, Cavanagh, & Gega, 2007; Norcross, 2006; Norcross et al., 2012). Most psychological reports can benefit by including suggestions for self-help or education regarding the problem being assessed. This is consistent with the finding that most psychologists use self-help as adjuncts to psychotherapy (Norcross, 2006). It is also common for the general public to use self-help resources even if they do not receive formal mental health treatment. The importance of this is highlighted in that the majority of people with diagnosable mental health conditions will not receive mental health care (WHO World Mental Health Survey Consortium, 2004). Thus, one of the most common ways people change is through self-help. Finally, it has been found that high-quality, well-implemented self-help interventions are nearly as effective as formal treatments administered by mental health professionals (effect sizes range between 0.50 and 0.80; Den Boer, Wiersma, & Van Den Bosch, 2004).

A major challenge in making recommendations for self-help is to determine which ones are likely to be beneficial. A valuable resource is Norcross et al.'s *Authoritative Guide to Self-Help Resources in Mental Health* (4th ed.; 2012). Resources are organized according to self-help books, autobiographies, Internet resources, films, and national support groups. Clinicians can be helped in deciding which resources to recommend by referring to survey-based ratings that rank the quality of the self-help materials.

Another valuable resource that lists, evaluates, and describes computer-aided psychotherapy is Marks et al.'s *Hands-on Help: Computer Aided Psychotherapy* (2007). Marks et al. also provide guidance on how clinics can obtain, support, screen, and implement computer-aided treatment. The PRWA includes a menu of self-help resources specific to each of the psychological report modules (personality, psychoeducational, forensic, etc.). The self-help resources are organized according to the type of problem or diagnoses the client is confronting (e.g., abuse, addiction, depression, divorce). Only those resources with the highest ratings were included in the PRWA program. Although this menu provides important options, clinicians are still encouraged to expand their knowledge of additional resources through consulting (Norcross, 2006; Norcross et al., 2012) as well as through reading and experimentation.

In addition to listing self-help resources in psychological reports, psychologists should also be prepared to offer suggestions on how these might be best implemented (see Norcross, 2006). One strategy is to assess the past experience clients have had with self-help. This will allow a greater understanding of what might be useful versus not useful as well as determining if self-help is even appropriate for a client. Some clients need self-help that simply provides information combined with clear instructions, whereas others might need self-help approaches that impact them more emotionally or focus on a more spiritual level. Sometimes clients are quite self-motivated, whereas others need considerable assistance. This means tailoring the recommendations not only to the type of problem but also to the unique characteristics of the person. For example, one way of phrasing a recommendation might be to simply state, "Have Ms. Jones read *Mastery of Your Anxiety and Panic III*." A more individualized way of phrasing this might be to write the following: "In order to reduce Mary's panic attacks, it is recommended that Ms. Jones read *Mastery of your Anxiety and Panic III*. This should be accompanied by weekly 15-minute consultations with Dr. Young to integrate the exercises, monitor the success, and motivate her to proceed to the next step of the self-help program."

Self-help often includes referral to support groups. There are a wide number of national organizations that can be contacted, such as the Learning Disabilities Association of America, Alchololics Anonymous, and Agoraphobics Building Independent Lives. Many of these have local chapters that provide regular meetings. An important strategy would be for psychologists to become familiar with these so they can make their referrals more specific to the community the client lives in. Two self-help Internet sites that provide information on local listings of support groups are http://mentalhelp.net/selfhelp/ and http://mhselfhelp.org/. A further strategy that greatly increases the likelihood the client will follow through with the referral would be to arrange for the meeting/appointment with the collaboration of the client and when the client is actually present. It can also sometimes help to contact a friend or family member who would be willing to accompany the client to the support group. If it is not appropriate for the assessing psychologists to do this, then they can incorporate suggestions for increasing adherence into the recommendations section of the report itself.

## Placement

In addition to treatment planning, clinicians often need to decide where the intervention will take place. These can involve either voluntary or involuntary settings. The typical treatment setting is an outpatient clinic that the client decides to attend. Additional voluntary options might include brief hospitalization, day hospitalization, residence in a group home, or a residence in a sober living environment. Involuntary (mandated) placements might include 24/7 observation, involuntary commitment to an inpatient facility, or guardianship. Forensic reports might also include subcategories of incarceration such as placement in a locked forensic psychiatric ward, incarceration with persons the same age as the person being evaluated, use of maximum protection protocols, or supermax confinement.

## Further Evaluation

Often, psychological assessment is one of a variety of assessment procedures. This is particularly the case in medical settings where the psychologist is typically one of a team of professionals who work together to evaluate the client's needs and coordinate with one another to provide the treatment. For example, a multidisciplinary pain program typically includes not only evaluation by a a psychologist, but also a physiatrist, physical therapist, speech therapist, social worker, and case manager. Often, the psychologist's contribution is given in a case conference in which multiple additional forms of assessment are integrated. Thus, the psychologist is in the position of referring to these professionals as well as integrating the results of their assessments. Academic and forensic settings are also typically multidisciplinary with the result that referrals among various professionals are both common and even expected.

Other settings are more individually oriented such that the psychologist may be the primary person doing the assessment. For example, psychologists in private practice might do a personality assessment with the expectation that this would lead to several sessions of therapeutic assessment. During the course of assessment, the assessing psychologist might discover that there could be medical, financial, or legal aspects to the case that need to be addressed. Accordingly, it might be appropriate to refer the client to other professionals, although this may not have been anticipated prior to the assessment. Referrals might include evaluation by a psychiatrist to determine possible need and type of psychotropic medication, vocational assessment to assist with career decisions, or neurological evaluation to determine if there is brain dysfunction that might be accounting for the client's problematic behavior.

## Alteration of Environment

Changing aspects of a client's environment is an effective and time-honored means of creating change. Within a neuropsychological context, this might involve placing reminders for a client through timers on medication, notices on a door, stove burners that turn off automatically after a certain length of time, or appointing a staff or family member to remind the client of important meetings. Referral for an assessment and interventions by occupational therapists can be extremely useful.

Psychoeducational reports are likely to deal with issues such as distractibility, conduct difficulties, or learning problems. Thus, accommodations to these difficulties might involve having a student sit in front of the class, removing distractions from areas of study, or developing lists that require either the student or teacher to check off any completed tasks to assure that assignments have been correctly completed. Changing the environment might also involve developing a classroom or home management program to reinforce specific types of desired behavior. In these cases, assessment should be behaviorally oriented and involve an understanding of the antecedents, behaviors, and consequences of relevant behaviors. Additional examples of altering a client's environment might include avoiding situations that could result in relapse or placing notices on the refrigerator that highlight self-affirmations, positive self-statements, or contracts made with the client's therapist.

### Miscellaneous

A number of recommendations do not seem to fit into any of the above categories. One example is specifying with whom the report should be shared. This may include requesting that the report be shared with relevant health care professionals or that the report not be shared with the client. Another possibility is that there were no recommendations for treatment given as there was no compelling evidence that the client has genuine cognitive or psychiatric problems. Two other examples are that the client wear a MedicAlert bracelet or that, due to the client's difficulties, he or she should not operate a motor vehicle.

# Recommended Reading

Groth-Marnat, G., Roberts, R., & Beutler, L. E. (2001). Client characteristics and psychotherapy: Perspectives, support, interactions, and implications. *Australian Psychologist, 36,* 115–121.

Jongsma, A. E., & Peterson, L. M. (2006). *The complete adult psychotherapy treatment planner* (4th ed.). Hoboken, NJ: Wiley.

Jongsma, A. E., Peterson, L. M. & McInnis, W. P. (2006). *The child psychotherapy treatment planner* (4th ed.). Hoboken, NJ: Wiley.

Norcross, J. C. (2006). Integrating self-help into psychotherapy: 16 practical suggestions. *Professional Psychology: Research & Practice, 37*, 683–693.

Norcross, J., Santrock, J. W., Campbell, L. F., Smith, T. P., Sommer, R., & Zuckerman, E. L. (2012). *Authoritative guide to self-help resources in mental health* (4th ed.). New York, NY: Guilford Press.

Sturmey, P., & Hersen, M. (2012). *Handbook of evidence-based practice in clinical psychology* (Vols. I and II). Hoboken, NJ: Wiley.

# CHAPTER 5

# Types of Psychological Reports

The five major categories of psychological reports are described in this chapter along with guidelines. These guidelines have been incorporated into the Psychological Report Writing Assistant (PRWA) and integrated into separate modules to assist with writing each category of report. A discussion of wider issues related to the contexts for the categories of reports is included in Chapter 2 of the *Handbook of Psychological Assessment*, 5th edition (Groth-Marnat, 2009a). Chapter 15 of the *Handbook of Psychological Assessment* provides actual examples of some of the categories of reports. However, the information included in this chapter is far more practical and focused in that it describes actual strategies for writing various types of report.

Although the five major categories of reports seem to roughly cover the major types of reports, it should be noted that the distinctions among reports is sometimes fluid and artificial. For example, it's sometimes difficult to determine the difference between a "cognitive" and a "neuropsychological" report. In addition, most of the types of reports (neuropsychological, personality, etc.) can be done for forensic purposes, and they thus become "forensic" reports. A further consideration is that each of the categories of reports can be focused on screening, diagnosis, progress, or problem solving (Sattler, 2008). This means that there can be further subcategories of reports. Despite the difficulty forming exact and clear categories, it is hoped that the information presented here will allow report writers to have greater depth of understanding as well as acquire specific strategies for writing most of the different categories of reports.

Typically, psychologists develop training and experience writing reports in one or two of the above report categories. For example, neuropsychologists typically write neuropsychological reports, and counseling psychologists most likely write personality or vocational reports. However, there are times when there may be overlap or lack of clarity regarding expertise with the result that a professional psychologist will write several different categories of reports. Sometimes general clinical psychologists will be called upon to not only do personality/psychiatric evaluations but may also do neuropsychological or forensic evaluations. In some cases, especially when working in rural settings, there may not be specialty psychologists who are available to do specific types of assessments. A general guide is that psychologists should not practice beyond their level of competence. This means that they should be able to recognize when they are going beyond their level of competence and refer out to specialists when necessary.

One of the most useful strategies in learning to write different types of reports is to read reports that are similar to the one the examiner is trying to write. Thus, the recommended reading section focuses on resources that include a wide number of actual reports as well as discussions of how the clinicians worked through the various cases. In addition, it's sometimes possible to find different types of reports by searching online. For example, forensic reports often can be found for topics such as "false confessions" or "not guilty by reason of insanity," or for high-profile cases such as Jeffrey Dahmer, Mike Tyson, or Ted Kaczynski.

## INTELLECTUAL/COGNITIVE REPORTS

The intellectual/cognitive report reviews various domains of cognitive functioning. It would typically involve integrating the results of a standard test of intelligence (e.g., Wechsler intelligence scales, Kaufman Assessment Battery for Children–II) along with supplementary tests for memory (e.g., Wechsler Memory Scales–IV), achievement (e.g., Wechsler Individual Achievement Test–III, Wide Range Achievement Test–IV), attention, or visual construction.

In some instances an intellectual assessment that focuses exclusively on cognitive abilities can be derived mainly from a test such as the Wechsler Adult Intelligence Scale–IV (WAIS-IV) or Woodcock Johnson Cognitive Battery–III. This type of evaluation usually stems from a referral question that asks, "What is this person's level of intellectual functioning?" or "What are the client's intellectual strengths and weaknesses?"

Such broad questions are typically accompanied by more specific requests for information (e.g., ability to benefit from an educational program or function independently). However, an intellectual assessment can also be crucial in many personality, forensic, or vocational evaluations. There is also considerable overlap between intellectual, neuropsychological, and psychoeducational evaluations (see below). However, one reason for listing intellectual assessments/reports separately is that they are often one of the first types of evaluations professionals in training are requested to write. In addition, general professional psychologists are quite likely to develop and be competent in performing general intellectual assessments. In contrast, specialists are more likely to be the ones performing the more in-depth and nuanced evaluations consistent within clinical neuropsychology.

As previously noted, referral questions for intellectual assessment typically have some questions that are fairly general such as assessing the person's cognitive strengths and weaknesses. However, there should also be quite specific questions such as the person's ability to benefit from a rehabilitation or educational program. These more specific questions relate to what the information might be used for. This often can be obtained by asking the referral sources what decisions need to be made regarding the examinee. The practical implication for report writers is that they should make sure that these specific, decision-relevant questions are included in the referral question section.

Another feature of reports summarizing intellectual assessment is that the background information section should include a focus on information directly relevant to the examinees' cognitive level of functioning. This would include academic history (grades, level of education, possible learning difficulties), vocational achievement (type and complexity of work), and medical history (presence of head injuries, exposure to neurotoxic substances). Particular emphasis should be placed on the client's history of recreational and prescription drug use since this might potentially impact a client's intellectual level of functioning. In contrast, personal/psychosocial and family history is typically less important, and this should be reflected in relatively shorter personal/psychosocial/family sections.

The interpretive domains for reports of intellectual functioning reflect a combination of those areas that have been assessed along with information relevant to the referral question (see Rapid Reference 5.1). Often, this is reflected in the domains/factors within the test itself. Thus, a report that relies heavily on the Wechsler intelligence scales would most likely include the following domains: general intellectual ability, verbal ability, perceptual reasoning, working memory, and processing speed. Because the Wechsler intelligence scales have only partial measures of memory, an additional test (e.g., Rey Auditory Verbal Learning Test) or a test battery (e.g., Wechsler Memory Scale–IV) may be used to make a more complete assessment of memory. A final common feature is to include a measure of achievement that assesses grade-level equivalent for reading, spelling, and arithmetic (Wide Range Achievement Test–4, Wechsler Individual Achievement Test–III). The three major areas of ability, memory, and achievement can be considered the three "pillars" of cognitive assessment.

---

### RAPID REFERENCE 5.1: COMMON FUNCTIONAL DOMAINS FOR AN INTELLECTUAL ASSESSMENT REPORT

- General intellectual ability
- Verbal ability
- Nonverbal ability
- Processing speed
- Working memory
- Memory
- Achievement

---

There are certainly other tests of intellectual ability that, due to their construction, would require a somewhat different listing of functional domains. For example, the Cognitive Assessment System (Das & Naglieri, 1994) has been developed according to Luria's Planning–Attention–Simultaneous–Successive (PASS) Model (Luria, 1973). As a result, the domains in the Impressions and Interpretations section for a report using the Cognitive Assessment System might follow the PASS model and include the following: general ability, planning, attention, simultaneous, successive. Having said this, it is also possible to interpret other tests, including the Wechsler intelligence scales according to the PASS model. Because the Wechsler intelligence scales are the most frequently used assessment tools, the domains presented in the PRWA follow the domains most closely associated with the Wechsler intelligence scales. However, practitioners using the software can certainly edit the existing domains or insert entirely new ones depending on the domains of interest combined with the cognitive tests that have been used.

The extent to which writers of cognitive reports include technical information to package their interpretations varies widely. A technically oriented report might include descriptions of confidence intervals ("90% confident that the scores would fall between 85 and 100"), comments on variability ("John's overall IQ of 110 masks a high degree of variability in his subtest profile"), detailing the practitioner's reasoning processes ("the discrepancy between these two indexes represents a significant difference between . . ."), and jargon ("crystalized intelligence was a relative strength"). In contrast to this approach is the emphasis in the PRWA on providing the end product of the interpretations in everyday, user-friendly language that describes the person rather than test scores. One of the features of the PRWA is the use of "red flag alerts" that help report writers identify that they have used quite technical, test-oriented language. These alerts provide a rationale for why it might be preferable to use more everyday language and, in many cases, suggest alternative language that will hopefully assist them in rewriting aspects of their reports in a more user-friendly nontechnical manner that focuses on the person rather than test scores or jargon.

A final guideline is to use strategies to expand interpretations to provide a full description of the person. Not all of these strategies would or even should be used for each domain. Instead, these strategies are merely a menu that report writers can pick and chose from. In some cases, it might be sufficient to merely make a quite succinct and general interpretation and not elaborate further ("the speed with which John is able to process information was in the average range"). In other situations, especially when the domain is crucial to the referral question, it might be important to expand on the interpretation in more detail. In these cases, the report writer might wish to utilize one or more of the following strategies:

1. Make an initial *general statement* ("excellent verbal abilities . . . ," etc.).
2. Elaborate by listing *subcomponents* ("good fund of general information, excellent word knowledge . . .").

3. Give a *qualitative description of test responses* ("could not recall more than five numbers that had been read to her" or "Ms. Jones did poorly on a series of questions asking her factual information related to history, science, and literature").
4. Give *qualitative descriptions of history/behavioral* observations ("she frequently needed to be reminded of the question that she had been asked").
5. Provide *implications for everyday life* ("she would have a difficult time recalling instructions that had been given to her").

An example of this strategy using information from the WAIS-IV and strategies 1, 3, and 5 is included below:

1. *General statement:* "Jane's ability to solve nonverbal problems was in the low average range (Perceptual Reasoning Index = 80 or the lower 6% of the population)."
3. *Qualitative description of test response:* "For example, she had a difficult time assembling a series of blocks that were given to her."
5. *Implications for everyday life:* "This suggests she would have a difficult time following maps or repairing simple machinery."

The preceding five-point strategy has been integrated into PRWA. These strategies are provided for cognitive interpretive domains and are available as menus of common phrases that can be inserted into a report. They are also included as guidelines for each cognitive domain and located in the bottom left window of the "compose template." Examples of behaviors for everyday life are described in the *Handbook of Psychological Assessment*, 5th edition in the descriptions of the indexes (Verbal Comprehension, p. 150; Perceptual Reasoning, p. 154; Working Memory, pp. 160–161; Processing Speed, p. 163).

## Neuropsychological Reports

As noted in the previous section, neuropsychological assessments are similar to cognitive assessments. As a result, many of the guidelines provided for cognitive assessment also apply to neuropsychological evaluation. However, neuropsychological evaluations are typically more extensive and in more depth, and the cognitive descriptions are more nuanced (see Groth-Marnat, 2000; Lezak, Howieson, Bigler, & Tranel, 2012). Often, they are related to understanding the impact of specific neurological conditions such as strokes, dementia, head injuries, exposure to neurotoxic substances, brain-related effects of substance abuse, learning disabilities, or neurological diseases (Parkinson's disease, cerebral vascular disease, tumors). As a result, neuropsychological assessments are more likely to occur within medical or educational settings. One useful distinction is that whereas a neurologist evaluates what the *brain* is doing, a neuropsychologist evaluates what the *person* is doing as a result of brain dysfunction. This means that much of the focus of a neuropsychological report is on helping to make decisions and develop treatment plans based on a client's ability to perform activities in his or her daily life.

There are typically a wide number of domains assessed by neuropsychological assessment. Usually, these include a statement of a client's general intellectual ability followed by descriptions of the client's attention, language, spatial abilities, memory, and executive functions. Often sensory–motor functions and speed of processing information are also evaluated (see Rapid Reference 5.2). These domains are used to organize the subsections of the Impressions and Interpretations section of the report. There are numerous tests to evaluate each of these domains (see Lezak et al., 2012; Strauss, Sherman, & Spreen, 2006) but most neuropsychologists have a core set of tests that they use with all or most clients (e.g., WAIS-IV, Wechsler Memory Scale–IV [WMS-IV], Neuropsychological Assessment Battery) and then include additional tests depending on which areas of functioning they are particularly interested in.

RAPID REFERENCE 5.2: COMMON FUNCTIONAL DOMAINS FOR A NEUROPSYCHOLOGICAL REPORT

- General intellectual ability
- Attention
- Language
- Spatial abilities
- Memory
- Executive functions
- Speed of processing
- Sensorimotor functions

A frequent issue with neuropsychological reports is they can easily include technical terms that many consumers will not comprehend. This is somewhat understandable in that clinical neuropsychology is usually embedded in the highly technical health care system such that it may seem natural to include technical language. This may include terms such as *postconcussive syndrome, visual neglect, agnosia,* or *aphasia.* If these and other technical terms are used, report writers should also consider writing clear descriptions in everyday language of what these terms mean. This is especially important if patients and other untrained persons are likely to read the report.

The length of neuropsychological reports can be quite variable. Sometimes the length will be only 1 to 2 pages if the purpose of the evaluation is to summarize ongoing trials to evaluate the effect of medication or readiness for rehabilitation, or to develop a baseline and follow-up for other procedures. Somewhat longer reports (3 to 6 pages) are required if the purpose of the evaluation is to assist with life planning or develop intervention strategies. The longest reports (10 to 20 pages) usually occur when neuropsychological evaluation is part of a forensic examination.

Most patients who are given neuropsychological assessments have some sort of brain-behavior condition that is likely to be apparent in their behavior. They may have word-finding difficulties or motor-sensory deficits, forget relevant information, or have a difficult time staying focused. Observations should be made for such things as the patient's capacity to take part in the interview and testing. Of particular interest is the extent and style the client understands and follows through on instructions. This means that his or her behavior during the assessment sessions can be quite rich and informative. Thus, clinicians need to be familiar with various neuropsychological conditions and observant with how these conditions may be expressing themselves in the client being evaluated. This should then be reflected in the Behavioral Observation section of the report.

A further particularly important feature of neuropsychological reports is that the Summary/Recommendations should be concise and yet sufficiently comprehensive to stand on its on. In other words, readers should be able to understand the essentials of the case by reading only the Summary and Recommendations. This is because neuropsychological reports are typically filed in client charts, where they will be briefly reviewed by a number of staff involved in the care and progress of the client. The importance of brevity is illustrated in that, in many inpatient settings, neuropsychological reports are limited to two pages.

Recommendations for neuropsychological reports need to integrate patient data and knowledge of interventions with the needs of the patient (see Lemsky, 2000). These can be used to restore function, develop tools to compensate for problems, alter the environment, and provide strategies to maximize behavioral change (Lemsky, 2000; Scherer, 2011). Within a cognitive rehabilitation context, Lemsky has provided a large number of "menu" items for the following domains:

- Memory and learning
- Verbal functioning
- Mental activities
- Visual–spatial/perceptual functioning
- Executive functioning

For example, a sample of recommendations from a neuropsychological report of a patient who has had a moderately severe traumatic brain injury might include the following:

> Cognitive rehabilitation should focus on (a) external memory compensation strategies including a memory diary, notes on a whiteboard, and alarms for medication and appointments; (b) internal memory strategies such as repeating things several times and PQRST (preview, question, read, self-recitation, test); (c) participation in a memory group focusing on support for using multiple techniques and social support to reduce the stress of having memory difficulties; (d) altering the environment by removing hazards/clutter; and (e) compensating for attentional difficulties by breaking complex tasks into simple ones, avoiding multitasking, and limiting distractions (noise, music, people talking, other nearby activities).

Many of these "menu" items have been included in the PRWA such that users of the software can select and edit these items. There are also many additional neuropsychologically relevant recommendations included in the PRWA that can be selected based on the referral question, assessment findings, needs of the client, and available resources.

## PSYCHOEDUCATIONAL REPORTS

Referrals for psychoeducational (academic) functioning are usually for school-age children or adolescents and may be initiated by teachers, parents, school administrators, physicians, or attorneys. Typical questions might be to understand such things as giftedness, poor grades, distractibility, difficulty with peer relations, and attention-seeking behavior. Although most psychoeducational evaluations are for children, it is increasingly common for academic evaluations to be requested by and for adults who are seeking consideration for attention-deficit disorder or learning disabilities. The eventual report can serve as a basis for developing academic interventions, to assist with program evaluation, as a baseline for future reference, and as a legal document (see Bradley-Johnson & Johnson, 2006).

Psychoeducational reports are usually written for schools and clinics. Each of these settings has somewhat different considerations. Schools are primarily concerned with how a child's or adolescent's learning, psychological, or developmental problems interfere with his or her ability to function and progress in school (Braaten, 2007). Thus, a school psychologist will want to know how and why a depressed child/adolescent is having academic difficulties. In contrast, a clinical evaluation is more likely to be broader in that a report will need to provide information on how a child/adolescent can be helped in a variety of settings. This means that a report describing a depressed child/adolescent should not only address school performance but also review issues involved in optimizing psychotherapy or recommending medication. A further difference is that school reports are used by a multidisciplinary team that can include school principals, general education teachers, special education teachers, nurses, psychologists, physical therapists, occupational therapists, and speech and language therapists. In contrast, clinical reports are written for a much narrower group of professionals. An additional difference is that school assessments require continual review of the children/adolescents to determine if they are still eligible for special consideration. In contrast, this is rarely needed for clinical evaluations.

One of the core issues for psychoeducational reports, especially for school settings, is to take into account the implications of the Individuals with Disabilities Act (IDEA). In order to qualify for free and appropriate education under the IDEA, children or adolescents must have a disability in areas such as a specific learning disability, traumatic brain injury, autism, visual/language impairment, hearing impairment, or intellectual disability (mental retardation). The report serves an essential gatekeeping function. This means report writers need to be clear on the diagnostic criteria, make sure the necessary criteria are present, and clearly state in the report that these criteria have (or have not) been met. If the qualifying criteria are present, the next step is to use the report to assist in developing an Individualized Education Program (IEP). Whereas the report is a crucial part of developing the IEP, the ultimate design is based on a team consisting of the child's parent, at least one teacher, a person who can supervise special instructions, and a person who can interpret the implications of the assessment results. Sometimes an additional person is included, such as a social worker who has essential information related to the child/adolescent. In some cases, the child/adolescent is also included. If the report will be used to inform an IEP, then the report writer needs to be sure to include the types of information that will be useful for possible inclusion in the IEP.

Whereas most types of reports include observations from outside sources, this is particularly crucial for psychoeducational reports. This is partially due to the fact that the client him- or herself is usually a child or adolescent, who are typically poor historians. The main people who contribute this information are teachers and parents, but it is also often helpful to obtain information from additional sources such as family members other than parents or physicians. This information is then combined with behavioral observations made during the assessment session itself. One issue that often comes up is that there may be discrepancies between observations made by the parent as opposed to how the child/adolescent describes his or her condition. Frequently, this is based on the child/adolescent having access to internal experiences such as anxiety or depression that a parent may not be aware of. Discrepancies can also occur between observations made by the school versus those made by the parent. It can often be useful to discuss and develop explanations as to why these differences occur.

The History/Background section of any psychoeducational report should emphasize developmental and academic information (see Braaten, 2007; Bradley-Johnson & Johnson, 2006). Developmental information may include the following: milestones for language, motor, and social development; milestones for adaptive skills; living arrangements/home environment; information about parents; and information about siblings. Academic information should include a combination of the following: early school experiences, highest grade completed, grades, hardest/easiest subject, any academic difficulties, any behavioral difficulties, schools attended, behavior in the classroom, record of attendance, grade in school, name of child/adolescent's teacher, methods of teaching in the classroom, learning style, interaction with the family in relation to school, any special education, and current or past use of medication. It is within the context of the above information that the interpretations and recommendations take on relevant meaning.

As with any type of report, the recommendations provide suggestions for how the presenting problem might be solved. They should be based on all information developed from the assessment, utilize available resources, and be realistic. Typically, four to six well-thought-out recommendations are sufficient. If too many are included, it may even be counterproductive in that they could overwhelm the reader, be confusing, and even reduce the likelihood that any of them would be acted on. However, sometimes referrals from schools do not want recommendations included in a report because it may then mean that the school is legally and financially required to implement the recommendations. Thus, it would be important to determine whether including recommendations in the report is something that is desired. Sattler (2008) has divided psychoeducational recommendations into the following categories (see also Rapid Reference 5.3):

1. *Environmental strategies* (e.g., adjust class schedules, change student's seating, increase structure of learning environment, provide small-group instruction).
2. *Organization/presentation/curriculum strategies* (e.g., allow extra time to complete assignments, shorten assignments, shorten work periods, simplify instructions, tailor instruction to student's learning style, use one-on-one tutorials, provide peer tutoring, combine both oral and visual instruction, ask student to repeat instructions to ensure understanding).
3. *Behavioral strategies* (e.g., develop behavioral contracts, use positive reinforcement, use negative consequences, provide immediate

feedback, prepare daily/weekly progress reports, train in anger control).

4. *Study skill strategies* (e.g., set short-term goals, survey material, develop questions, identify relevant facts, review material, have student check work and test him- or herself).

5. *School–parent strategies* (e.g., develop home/school communication system, have parent write contract with child/adolescent, create parent–child reward system, use flash cards, have student explain homework to parent, implement home reward system, have parent review homework, have parent communicate with teacher weekly).

The preceding categories of recommendations, including specific recommendations themselves, are available as a menu format integrated into the PRWA.

## RAPID REFERENCE 5.3: CATEGORIES OF PSYCHOEDUCATIONAL RECOMMENDATIONS

- Change environment.
- Reorganize presentation format and/or curriculum.
- Alter child's behavior.
- Improve study skills.
- Improve/integrate school/parent communication.

## PERSONALITY REPORTS

The "personality" report is most frequently found in settings that are concerned with understanding not only personality itself but also various types and levels of psychopathology. As a result, these reports are typically written in and for psychiatric and psychological clinics. Topics might include developing an understanding of a person's range of personality functioning (both positive and problematic), style of coping, quality of his thought processes, motivations that organize and direct his behavior, and the quality and level that he understands himself and other people. Consistent with these topics are referral questions that ask what type of treatment the person could most benefit from, how he will cope under stress, what can be done to overcome an impasse in therapy, what his patterns in relationships are, why he has difficulty expressing emotions, or what his diagnosis is.

An issue that is particularly challenging in personality assessment is to expand and integrate the test scores in such a way as to give life to the person and present a compelling narrative. Whereas this is an issue for any type of report, it becomes particularly crucial for personality assessment. One general stance is for the practitioner to articulate a sense of the client's experience of the world. This would mean that instead of a scale elevation having a simple mechanical relation to the interpretive descriptions provided, the practitioner also needs to think about how that person sees the world and how his way of coping makes sense to the person being evaluated. Some authors have developed useful guides that provide client feedback and interpretive statements that use everyday language, empathize with the client, and are designed to facilitate client change (Finn, 2007; Finn, Fischer, & Handler, 2012; Fischer, 2012; Levak, Siegel, Nichols, & Stolberg, 2011). Interpretations based on these sources can be extracted, integrated, edited, and inserted into the report.

Another strategy is to use models of client functioning. The main focus of these models is to provide a list and description of domains that provide the frame of the Impressions and Interpretations (Discussion) section. For example, the following domains might be considered important for a full description of personality: cognitive, emotional, interpersonal, coping style, and self-concept. Another strategy would be to describe the biological, psychological, and social aspects of the person being assessed. A final model divides the areas of functioning into the following five primary structures: thinking/information processing, emotion/affect processing, self-concept/ identity, interpersonal/social, awareness/regulation (Blais & Smith, 2008).

One useful strategy is to have a framework for expanding on personality interpretations. This is similar to the five strategies used for cognitive assessment (see Rapid Reference 5.4). Accordingly, not all of these would be used for any interpretive domain, but rather they would be used depending on the importance of elaborating on the domain, available information, referral question, and the desired length of the report.

1. Make an initial *general statement* ("high level of introversion").
2. Elaborate by listing the various *subcomponents* of what this means ("the client is reserved, reflective, low key, private, quiet, enjoys solitude, prefers one-to-one interaction").

3. Give *qualitative description of test responses* (incomplete sentences: "*I often feel. . .* overwhelmed when I'm around too many people" or the Thematic Apperception Test [TAT]: "Themes to stories told by the client indicated a need for solitude, reflection, spirituality").

4. Give *qualitative descriptions of history/behavioral observations* ("the client lives alone and prefers to have a few close friends" or "when asked questions, the client often remained silent for a short time as he considered how best to answer").

5. Provide *implications for everyday life* ("when under stress, the client prefers to be alone").

A full paragraph for the preceding set of interpretations on introversion would then read as follows:

Ms. Smith tends to be quite introverted, which means that she is reserved, low key, private, and quiet; enjoys solitude; and prefers one-to-one interaction more than being with large groups. For example, when asked to complete the sentence beginning with *I often feel*, she stated, "overwhelmed when I'm around too many people." In addition, she often stopped and took some time to reflect on the interview questions before she answered them. One of the implications for Ms. Smith's real-life functioning is that when under stress she would prefer to be alone.

---

RAPID REFERENCE 5.4: STRATEGIES FOR EXPANDING PERSONALITY INTERPRETATIONS

1. General statement of personality construct
2. Subcomponents of personality construct
3. Qualitative description of test response to illustrate personality
4. Qualitative description illustrating personality taken from history/behavioral observations
5. Implications for everyday life

---

As mentioned previously, personality assessment is often used to assist with clarifying a person's diagnosis. In some respects, knowledge of personality is quite useful in that it helps to understand the processes or structure that led a person to experience distress. If a personality disorder is part of the diagnosis, then personality assessment is, of course, crucial. In other types of diagnoses, personality assessment is not as important, especially when diagnosing Axis I disorders. This means that professional psychologists will need to rely much more on a careful history that includes not only the nature of the symptoms but also their onset, duration, severity, and frequency. But the crucial strategy of any diagnosis is carefully obtaining and lining up relevant criteria with the available assessment information. Thus, any practitioner should be able to not only provide the diagnosis but also to list why each one of the criteria for that diagnosis is present for the person being evaluated.

At the core of any person's functioning is the interplay between her difficulties and her strengths. Thus, a complete personality description should acknowledge and expand on both of these sides of the person (Snyder, Ritschel, Rand, & Berg, 2006). For example, clients who are struggling with depression are likely to be self-critical, have thoughts related to hopelessness, and be quite sensitive to criticism. At the same time, they may have a strong sense of integrity and the ability to connect with other people on a deep level. Knowing these positive features helps with treatment planning, as it is often an expansion on their strengths that enables clients to improve. Indeed, numerous evidence-based procedures have been developed and focus on enhancing clients' strengths as a means of overcoming their difficulties (O'Hanlon & Bertolino, 2012; Snyder, Lopez, & Pedrotti, 2011). Including client strengths also does justice to the full complexity of a person. A further issue is that clients are quite likely to obtain and read copies of reports that have been written about them. If these reports follow a more medical model deficit approach in which positive features are not included, it is likely to be not only demoralizing but also antitherapeutic. Thus, practitioners should be aware of client assets, assess for these, and include them in a report by adding a section on client strengths.

A final crucial feature of writing a personality report is to articulate the distinction between explicit aspects of the person versus more implicit, hidden qualities. Explicit aspects of the person are typically derived from how a person describes him- or herself. This may be derived partially by asking for a self-description during interview ("How would you describe yourself?") but is mainly developed from responses to self-report measures such as the Minnesota Multiphasic Personality Inventory (MMPI-2/MMPI-2 RF) or Psychological Assessment Inventory. In contrast, implicit inferences are mainly derived from a combination of performance-based measures (Rorschach, TAT, sentence completion), noting the often hidden patterns of relationships, and inferring how a person relates to his environment. For example, a person might perceive himself as being highly virtuous and conscientious. This may be reflected in how the person describes himself. In contrast, his patterns of relationships and narratives to ambiguous images may reflect underlying resentment and using others for his personal gratification. Thus, these contradictory descriptions would need to be taken into account when describing various aspects of the person. Often, such differing perspectives can also help to interpret and explain what may on the surface appear to be contradictions in test data.

## FORENSIC REPORTS

Forensic evaluations focus on such areas as competence to stand trial, documentation of injury to determine compensation, not guilty by reason of insanity, level of dangerousness, risk of reoffending, ability to make legal decisions, ability to live independently, the possibility that a false confession may have occurred, or to assist with decisions related to child custody (see Heilbrun, Grisso, & Goldstein, 2008; Otto & Heilbrun, 2002; see also Rapid Reference 5.5). Many legal processes become adversarial. As a result, reports that are written within legal contexts are frequently subjected to extensive scrutiny. This is proper given that often the results of legal decisions can have quite significant consequences. In addition, forensic evaluations focus on quite specific areas and occur within a context that is often quite different from the typical psychological evaluation. This means that professional psychologists writing reports in legal contexts need to be aware of some of the specific issues that will arise and should be integrated into their reports (see Buchanan, Binder, Norko, & Swartz, 2012; Grisso, 2010; Worthen & Moering, 2012). In order to ensure that all relevant components are included, Witt (2010) has provided a useful forensic report checklist based on the most frequent deficiencies encountered in reports (see http://forensicpsychologyunbound. ws/-2010.2:233-240). As a result of the scrutiny and importance related to forensic reports, it is incumbent on assessors to develop and use the highest level of professional competence (see American Psychological Association, 2013).

### RAPID REFERENCE 5.5: COMMON TOPICS FOR FORENSIC REPORTS

- Competence to stand trial
- Personal injury
- Not guilty by reason of insanity
- Level of dangerousness
- Risk of reoffending
- Capacity to make legal decisions
- Ability to live independently
- False confession
- Child custody

One important area of knowledge is that numerous forensic-specific instruments have been developed. Some relevant examples include the MacArthur Competence Assessment Tool (Poythress et al., 1999), Evaluation of Competency to Stand Trial–Revised (Rogers, Tillbrook, & Sewell, 2004), Historical–Clinical–Risk Management–20 (HCR-20): Assessing Risk of Violence (Webster, Douglas, Eaves, & Hart, 1997), Uniform Child Custody Evaluation System (Munsinger & Karlson, 1994), and the Miller Forensic Assessment of Symptoms Test (Miller, 2001). These are frequently used to supplement more general traditional instruments such as the WAIS-IV, Millon Clinical Multiaxial Inventory–III (MCMI-III), or the MMPI-2/MMPI-2-RF (see Archer, 2006; Archer, Buffington-Vollum, Stredny, & Handel, 2006).

The format of forensic reports is typically fairly similar to the generic format found in other types of reports. However, additional headings may need to be included for validity, legal history, review of records, quality of relationship with parents, and competence-related abilities. These will typically be defined based on a combination of the referral question and the types of instruments that have been selected. For example, the validity of assessment is frequently a core issue when plaintiffs/defendants may stand to gain by either exaggerating or mini-mizing their problems. This means that practitioners should spend some time dealing with the validity of their results through integrating the results of relevant behaviors, relevant records, validity scales, and the results of specialized instruments to detect malingering such as the Miller Forensic Assessment of Symptoms Test (Miller, 2001) or the Test of Memory Malingering (Tombaugh, 1996).

The format also varies slightly for the interpretation of results and the summary. In most psychological reports there is a section titled "Impressions and Interpretations." However, using the term *impressions* sounds too speculative for the forensic arena. As a result, this section is often referred to as simply "Findings" or "Results." In addition, the con-cluding sections of forensic reports usually have a section called "Legal Issues," where the report writer provides his or her "opinions." This is usually included either instead of the Summary, or as a portion of the Summary where the referral questions are answered. Finally, many foren-sic reports do not include a Recommendations section unless recommen-dations have been specifically requested by the referral source.

---

**RAPID REFERENCE 5.6: KEY CHARACTERISTICS OF FORENSIC REPORTS I**

- Focus exclusively on legal questions asked by the referral source
- Usually designate examinee as plaintiff/defendant (not "client")
- Use of forensic-specific instruments
- Additional headings: validity, legal history, review of records, competence/ capacity to perform certain activities, child–parent relationships
- Translate legal/psychiatric terms into everyday language

---

One special case for the inclusion of prescribed content is a child cus-tody evaluation (see Ackerman, 2006). Because these are frequently quite contentious, the American Psychological Association (APA) has defined essential content that should be included and these are available online (www.apa.org/practice/childcustody) and in relevant publica-tions (*Guidelines for Psychological Evaluations in Child Protection Matters* [APA

Committee on Professional Practice and Standards, 1998] and *Guidelines for Psychological Evaluations in Divorce Proceedings* [APA, 1994]). A further useful resource is *Evaluation of Parenting Capacity in Child Protection* (Budd, Clark, & Connell, 2011). This is part of a comprehensive best practices series in forensic mental health assessment that includes relatively short (150 to 200 pages) guidebooks on areas including competence to stand trial, criminal responsibility, capacity to confess, sexually violent predators, risk of violence, capacity to consent to treatment, personal injury, civil commitment, workplace disability, and child custody (see Heilbrun, 2009; Heilbrun et al., 2008; Packer, 2009; Witt, 2009; Zapf & Roesch, 2009). Each book has a final chapter that provides clear, specific guidelines on report writing.

Forensic reports vary greatly in length. This is mediated to a large extent by the type of forensic report. For example, capacity to stand trial evaluations vary between 1 and 15 pages, with average lengths being between 4 and 5.5 pages (Christy, Douglas, Otto, & Petrila, 2004; Heilbrun & Collins, 1995). In contrast, child custody reports range between 5 and 63 pages, with an average of 24 pages (Bow et al., 2002). The greater length for child custody reports is due to the greater complexity (number of people and settings), and this complexity is reflected in the more extensive content required by the above child custody guidelines.

Any report should begin with an identification of the examinee. However, it should be noted that the examinee is rarely referred to as a "client" but they are typically referred to as either the "plaintiff" or the "defendant." This is the case at the top of the report where the examinee is first designated, as well as throughout the narrative of the report itself.

Like most other reports, forensic evaluations begin with a statement of the referral question. However, there are a number of additional features and content areas that often need to be included (see Grisso, 2010; Witt, 2010). In addition to the referral question, there is also a statement of the legal issue (e.g., "Does the defendant have a psychiatric disorder that would have made it difficult for him to control his behavior?") and quite possibly a repeat of the legal standard (e.g., definition of insanity in the state where the trial is taking place). It is also crucial to stress that the report should focus only on the legal questions asked by the referral source. It is also prudent to translate technical legal or psychiatric terms into everyday language (Grisso, 2010). Underlying this guideline is that there should be an awareness that reports should be written for nonclinical readers as well as to meet the demands of legal forums.

Forensic reports require far more documentation than evaluations done in other contexts. Thus, information should be included for all sources of data (dates, who wrote/provided them, title of the data source), where the evaluation occurred, and times/places where any contacts were made. It is also crucial to provide multiple sources of information to strengthen the conclusions of the examiner. For example, a plaintiff for a personal injury case may present himself as existing in a semivegetative state, but sources from informants may indicate that he is successfully doing informal work. This reliance on sources other than merely tests results is far more important in forensic evaluations than for most other types of assessment.

The crux of the legal report is to provide opinions and to detail how the opinions were made. This is different from most other evaluations in which the referral sources are likely to be much more focused on the end product of the assessment process. The reason for this is that the psychologists' reasoning processes in forensic settings are likely to be challenged by the opposing counsel. Thus, forensic examiners may need to provide greater detail regarding their reasoning processes when compared to other types of evaluations. The Integrated Information Manager in the PRWA provides an ideal format for organizing this information. For example, a practitioner may conclude that the plaintiff is exaggerating his or her symptoms. The practitioner can easily look at the grid where he made notes relating to symptom exaggeration and list the various sources he used to come to this conclusion. During this process, it is crucial to be clear on the difference between facts ("The injury occurred on September 2, 2010, in the plaintiff's office . . ."), data ("F score of 98 on the MMPI-2"), and opinions ("The plaintiff was exaggerating his level of impairment.").

A further recommendation with forensic reports is to include all the data. Thus, a person reviewing the report can potentially assess if the author was "cherry picking" the data to support preferred arguments of the author. It is also advised to not only provide evidence for why the assessor came to the conclusions (e.g., "Based on the following information, the plaintiff has a high risk of reoffending") but to also include contrary evidence ("Some data that are contrary to this opinion are . . .").

This assures the reader that a variety of possibilities were considered prior to coming to the final opinion. The result is to increase the objectivity of the opinion and potentially defuse counterarguments that the opposing counsel may have to the opinions included in the report. In other words, the counterarguments have not only been considered, but they have been discarded as not being sufficiently persuasive to have changed the report writer's opinions.

A final guideline that is particularly important in forensic reports is to not overstate the opinions/interpretations (Grisso, 2010; Witt, 2010). For example, sometimes practitioners may incorrectly state that the person being assessed has had a "loss of memory" or is "unable to control his behavior." Both of these statements are unlikely to be true. No one has a "loss of memory," but instead he has "difficulties" with his memory or he has "mild/moderate/severe memory impairment." Similarly, a person is rarely "unable to control his behavior," but he instead has "difficulty" controlling his behavior. Finally, it is unlikely that a person being assessed "does not understand the trial process," but, in contrast, there may be *aspects* of the trail process that he does understand versus those that he does not understand. Thus, a more nuanced description as suggested in the preceding examples is likely to be more credible, accurate, and useful. In addition, overstating conclusions potentially opens the report writer to being discredited by the opposing counsel.

---

**RAPID REFERENCE 5.7: KEY CHARACTERISTICS OF THE FORENSIC REPORT II**

- Detailed documentation required
- Detail how opinions were made
- Distinction among facts, data, and opinions
- Include contrary evidence
- Do not overstate opinions/interpretations

---

## VOCATIONAL/CAREER REPORTS

Vocationally oriented reports are prepared to either assist a person in determining an appropriate career direction or to help organizations make optimal decisions regarding hiring or promoting an employee. Each of these considers a range of somewhat different issues. A person exploring career directions may be uncertain regarding which career would be best for her. This may be due to current struggles with decisions regarding various options, unhappiness with a current occupation, needing to satisfy recommendations from others, confirming that her career choice is the best one, or to determine if she is truly ready for a career change. In contrast, organizations may wish to use information in a vocational report to choose between two or more candidates. The information may help to understand the applicant's style of management, how she solves problems, what she does when under stress, or to better understand the applicant's cognitive style. Given that minimal research and guidelines have not yet been developed for vocational reports, they have not been included in the PRWA. However, a discussion of relevant issues is included in this section to assist report writers who might be interested in this area.

It is particularly crucial that vocational reports, especially those prepared for clients seeking career direction, be written in a clear, user-friendly style. This is because the client him- or herself will be the main one to read the report. This means that careful attention needs to be given to how the client might assimilate the report. The report might talk directly to the person using such phrases as "This report has been written to help you carefully consider . . ." or "This report will provide a written record of your abilities and personality related to. . . ." It may take a client a year or more to fully assimilate the results and implications of the report. In addition, the report may be an accompaniment to 3 to 4 hours of counseling in which the professional psychologist provides counseling related to the results. The report itself, then, becomes a tool to refresh what was discussed and to carefully consider the implications of the assessment over an extended period of time.

Perhaps the key feature of a vocational report is to articulate the degree of fit between the client and a variety of possible careers. It is understood, however, that a perfect fit is rarely possible, but it is the goal of the client and the report writer to provide options that are as close a fit as possible. A possible scenario might read something like the following:

Mr. Smith is a 28-year-old, married, Asian American male who was pursuing a degree in engineering as a result of parental pressure as his parents wanted to make sure that he had secure, well-paying employ-ment. He was self-referred for career assessment because he had been experiencing work dissatisfaction. . . .

It is the job of the report writer to point out the possible impact of external pressure to pursue a certain career and to provide different options. Another client might have unrealistic expectations regarding the financial rewards, opportunities for advancement, or degree of satisfaction of a career. Finally, another person might have an excellent personality and ability match for a career, but there may be clinical difficulties such as depression or a passive aggressive style that are interfering with his or her ability to advance and achieve career satisfaction. In each of these cases, the report writer needs to state the opportunities and conflicts by matching the degree of fit the client has for various careers.

In providing assessment information it is not the job of the report writer to provide definitive statements of whether or not a client should pursue a specific career. However, it is the job of the report writer to indicate that, if she does attempt to pursue a particular career that is not a good fit, then it is likely to be quite challenging for her. For example, an introvert who wishes to pursue a career that requires a high degree of constant interaction with a wide number of people may find the work particularly draining. Another example might be a person who is not particularly good with details such that he may have a quite difficult time pursuing a career in law or accounting. Thus, a phrase such as the following may be appropriate: ". . . This does not rule out a career in accounting, but you would be likely to find it quite difficult to become proficient." This can often be done by comparing the client's scores on tests with a particular reference group (i.e., "Your scores on a test measur-ing the extent you focus on details was in the lower 5% compared with other persons who pursue careers in accounting"). The challenge is to never completely eliminate a career as an option but, given the assessment results, to invite further opportunities for self-exploration.

The main domains for the impressions/interpretations section of a vocational report are abilities, interests, and personality (Lowman, 1991; see Rapid Reference 5.8). These provide coverage of most of the areas relevant for persons seeking vocational guidance. Abilities are rela-tively stable aspects of the person that have implications for a person's likelihood that he will be proficient at doing certain things. The broadest assessment of ability is the global or full-scale IQ. There is ample research that this is one of the best predictors of both academic and vocational success (Schmidt & Hunter, 1998, 2004). However, success is also dependent on more specific abilities. For example, an attorney would need to have excellent verbal abilities, but his or her nonverbal abilities may be far less crucial. In contrast, an architect would need to have superior nonverbal abilities. Thus, a client's relative cognitive strengths and weaknesses allows for a more nuanced means of evaluating the fit between abilities and a potential career.

---

**RAPID REFERENCE 5.8: COMMON FUNCTIONAL DOMAINS FOR A VOCATIONAL ASSESSMENT**

- Abilities
- Interests
- Personality

---

There are numerous abilities, along with a correspondingly high number of tests to measure these abilities. Abilities might be reflected in the pattern of scores measured on a test such as the WAIS-IV (verbal abilities, perceptual reasoning, speed, attention/working memory). Additional tests might be administered to evaluate such abilities as mechanical reasoning, musical ability, aesthetic judgment, emotional intelligence, computational abilities, creative imagination, or memory. As a general rule, a person should score in the top 25% of the population in order for the ability to be considered a strength that is high enough to suggest that they might do well in a specific career. In the example of the architect and the attorney, a report writer would want the architect to score in the top 25% of the population in nonverbal abilities and a possible attorney to score in the top 25% for verbal abilities.

Just because a person has a good fit between his pattern of abilities and a career does not then mean that he will have an interest in that area.

This means that that it is crucial to determine if a client has interests in certain areas. Interests essentially measure the types of work that a person finds appealing. Interests can be informally assessed through simply asking the person what careers he has considered or to ask him for occupational daydreams he might have had. He might also be asked what it is that he *really* wants to do. More formal assessment can be through an interest inventory such as the Strong Vocational Interest Blank or the Self-Directed Search.

A final crucial component is the degree to which the client's personality fits various careers. For example, a research scientist is usually introverted, conscientious, and curious. There are also subspecialties within careers that have implications for personality. This can be illustrated in that the qualities that make a good trial attorney (e.g., comfortable with adversarial situations, extroverted) may not be the same as an attorney who is primarily concerned with research and document preparation (e.g., introverted, comfort with adversarial relationships is not as important). Important personality dimensions that might be considered in a career report include dominance, flexibility, the extent the person expresses feelings, degree to which the person focuses on thinking (is cerebral), introversion/extroversion, intuitiveness, conscientiousness, openness, problem-solving style, coping style, and level of adjustment. These can be measured by common personality tests such as the NEO Personality Inventory–3 (NEO-PI-3), Psychological Assessment Inventory, California Psychological Inventory, Rorschach, or the Myers-Briggs Type Indicator.

One core issue to consider is potential clinical problems. If a person is experiencing burnout, has problems with substance abuse, or has difficulty empathizing with others, he will most likely experience career-related problems. This may be true even if there is an excellent fit between abilities, interests, and most aspects of personality. The person may mistakenly think that she is in the wrong career when a more important focus should be on resolving the clinical issues. In some cases, a change within the same career (e.g., less stress) may help rather than seeking a completely different career. Frequently, however, counseling may be the optimal intervention to resolving the clinical issues. This may or may not eventually result in the person's seeking a new career.

# Recommended Reading

Ackerman, M. J. (2006). *Clinician's guide to child custody evaluations* (3rd ed.). Hoboken, NJ: Wiley.

Braaten, E. B. (2007). *The child clinician's report writing handbook*. New York, NY: Guilford Press.

Bradley-Johnson, S., & Johnson, C. M. (2006). *A handbook for writing effective psycho-educational reports* (2nd ed.). Austin, TX: Pro-Ed.

Budd, K. S., Clark, J., & Connell, M. A. (2011). *Evaluation of parenting capacity in child protection*. New York, NY: Oxford University Press.

Heilbrun, K. (2009). *Evaluation for risk of violence in adults*. New York, NY: Oxford University Press.

Heilbrun, K., Grisso, T., & Goldstein, A. (2008). *Foundations of forensic mental health assessment*. New York, NY: Oxford University Press.

Heilbrun, K., Marczyk, G. G., & Dematteo, D. (2002). *Forensic mental health assessment: A casebook*. New York, NY: Oxford University Press.

Lowman, R. L. (in press). *The clinical practice of career assessment: Interests, abilities, personality* (2nd ed.). Washington, DC: American Psychological Association.

Morgan, J. E., Baron, I. S., & Ricker, J. H. (Eds.). (2010). *Casebook of clinical neuropsychology*. New York, NY: Oxford University Press.

Packer, I. K. (2009). *Evaluation of criminal responsibility*. New York, NY: Oxford University Press.

Witt, P. H. (2009). *Evaluation of sexually violent predators*. New York, NY: Oxford University Press.

Witt, P. H. (2010). Forensic report checklist. *Open Access Journal of Forensic Psychology, 2*, 233–240; http://forensicpsychologyunbound.ws/-2010.2:233-240

Zapf, P. A., & Roesch, R. (2009). *Evaluation of competence to stand trial*. New York, NY: Oxford University Press.

# CHAPTER 6

# PRWA Overview and Sample Walkthrough

## INTRODUCTION

This chapter provides a brief overview to the main features of the Psychological Report Writing Assistant (PRWA). We hope using the software will be smooth, easy, and intuitive, and help you write comprehensive, user-friendly psychological reports. Although this chapter provides an overview, a more detailed set of instructions can be found in the User Manual that is associated with the Help functions of the software.

It should first be noted that not all the PRWA resources need to be used. Some may find the common phrases the most useful and decide not to use some of the other resources. In contrast, others may find the menu of recommendations and Integrated Information Manager to be much more useful and will therefore focus on these. It is recommended that users review and experiment with all the various resources to determine which ones they feel are most useful, given their needs and report writing style.

As noted previously, the format and style of report writing emphasized in the PRWA have been derived from a thorough review of research combined with extensive feedback from clinical practice. As such, PRWA ideally presents what seems to be an optimal format and style of report writing. However, many professional psychologists will have developed their own variations on report writing. PRWA can easily accommodate these variations by the report writers editing sections of the report in the composition window—adding, modifying, and deleting various headings and their associated text blocks. In addition, PRWA allows users to develop their own customized report format. However, this may mean that various guidelines and resources provided in PRWA may not be available. For example, PRWA emphasizes and provides tools to assist with integrating interpretations according to domains (e.g., verbal abilities, coping style, etc.). If psychologists choose to develop their own customized reports, it may mean that some of the resources available for some of the sections of a report included in PRWA will not be relevant. For example, if users develop a customized report that includes an Impressions and Interpretations section that lists the findings according to tests/procedures (e.g., Minnesota Multiphasic Personality Inventory [MMPI-2-RF], Wechsler Intelligence Scale for Children–IV [WISC-IV]), then the common phrases developed for domains will not be available. Despite this, there will still be many features of PRWA that will be quite relevant, such as common phrases for other sections of the report (e.g., behavioral observations) or the menu of recommendations. PRWA does include a Wizard that allows the report writer to select any number of psychological tests and procedures as the headings for a custom report template that includes a section on findings according to tests/procedures. Additionally, PRWA provides a Generic Wizard that presents a hierarchical menu system making available all of PRWA's text reference resources, should the report writer want to search, insert, and then modify a relevant paragraph from the PRWA library. The templates for the five standard report types can thus be used as a starting point. From this basis, the user can then modify the format, content, and sequence of report headings and text blocks to create whatever template is desired for future use. Please see "Designing and Using Custom Report Templates" at the end of the User Manual.

A crucial assumption for report writing is that reading how other clinicians have written a report can often be a powerful means of understanding how a new and similar report can be written. This is likely to be especially true for professionals in training as well as experienced professionals who are writing a new type of report for the first time. For example, many clinical psychologists may have written numerous personality or cognitive reports but are now facing the new challenge of writing their first forensic reports. Thus, the PRWA software has examples, guidelines, recommendations, and so on for each of the five reports that have been described previously (see Chapter 5).

## DEVELOPING A PSYCHOLOGICAL REPORT WITH THE PRWA WIZARDS

To facilitate developing different types of psychological reports, PRWA provides a toolbar containing various Wizards. The following screenshot lists each of the Wizards.

These Wizards are context sensitive in that relevant Wizard command buttons become available when working on different sections of the

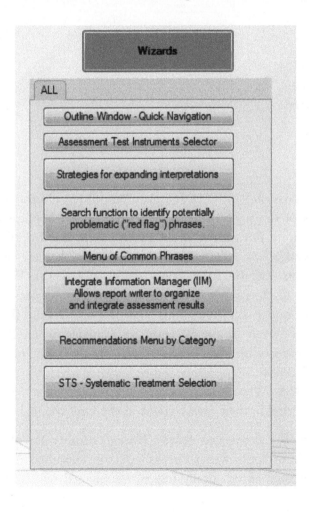

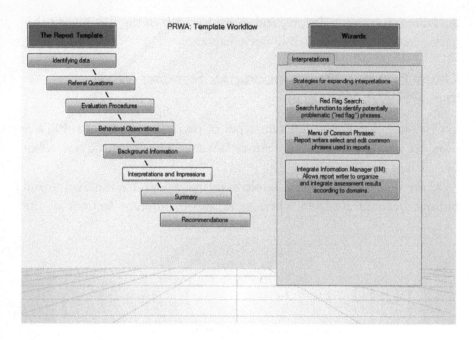

report. The screenshot (PRWA Template Workflow) illustrates the different sections of the report and the Wizards that are applicable for each of these sections. For example, the PRWA Template Workflow screenshot displayed above demonstrates the Wizards that are available for the Impressions and Interpretations section of a report. These Wizards will only be displayed when the report writer is working on one of the sections under Interpretations and Impressions in the template. Definitions for each of the Wizards are available when PRWA users place their cursors on the Wizards listed on the right of the PRWA Template Workflow.

The PRWA Wizards are briefly introduced next, and will be described in detail in their own sections in the User Manual.

*Assessment Test Instruments Selector Wizard.* From a list of test instruments, the report writer checks [√] the tests used for the client. PRWA then automatically inserts the selected tests into the report template.

*Menu of Common Phrases Wizard.* Report writers select, insert, and edit common phrases used in reports.

*Integrated Information Manager (IIM).* Allows the report writer to organize and integrate assessment results according to domains (functions described in the User Manual but not in the brief walkthrough included in this chapter).

*Recommendations Menu Wizard.* Allows the report writer to select recommendation(s) that will be automatically inserted into the report for editing.

*"Red Flag" Search Wizard.* Search function to identify potentially problematic (red flag) phrases.

*Systematic Treatment Selection (STS) Wizard.* Allows report writers to rate client characteristics most relevant to treatment planning and to then tailor treatments in order to optimize outcomes (functions described in the User Manual but not in the brief walkthrough included in this chapter).

*Spell-check.* Allows writers to check for possible spelling errors (functions described in the User Manual but not in the brief walkthrough included in Chapter 6).

## SAMPLE WALKTHROUGH: CREATING A NEW CLIENT RECORD AND DEVELOPING A PSYCHOLOGICAL REPORT

When you first launch the PRWA, you will see a sample client record in the directory, listed as **Neuropysch, Joe Allen (N)**. Reviewing this report will enable you to understand many of the features of PRWA. In the current walkthrough, you will see how to create a new client record, and specify a neuropsychological report to be developed for that client and modeled after Joe Neuropsych.

### Program Security

After you launch PRWA, the program security screen will be displayed, prompting you for your User Name and Password, which will be sent to you upon registration.

Type in your **User Name** and **Password**, then Click on the **[Login]** button to enter the program.

The main application console will then be displayed:

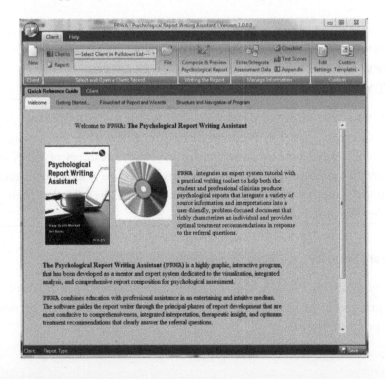

## Creating a New Client Record

To create a new client record, click on the **[New]** button in the leftmost part of the PRWA main ribbon bar:

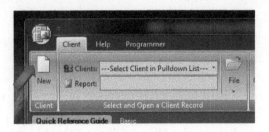

## Enter Client Identifying Information

In the "PRWA–Add New Client" window, pull down the "Type of Report" list box and select a report type for the client. In this example, we are composing a **Neuropsychological** report.

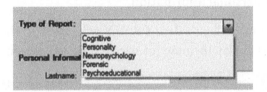

Type of Report

Enter the remaining information for the client. For the walkthrough, we will develop a neuropsychological report for Mary Janet Thompson. Her identifying information is typed in as follows:

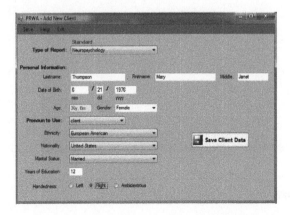

Add New Client

Please note that for Pronoun to Use, Gender, Ethnicity, Nationality, and Marital Status, you will pull down the respective list boxes for the valid options.

List boxes are signified by the downward array at the end of the field: For example:

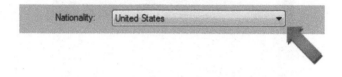

Nationality

When finished, click on the **[Save Client Data]** button.

Save Client Data

## Viewing Client Personal Information

After saving the new client's data, PRWA will return to the main application console and display the new (or selected) client's personal information.

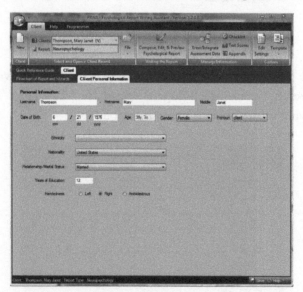

Client Personal Info

You are now ready to work on the report.

## Starting to Work on the Psychological Report

For this walkthrough, we will go directly to compose the psychological report by working with the template for neuropsychology reports.

Click on the large [**Compose, Edit, & Preview Psychological Report**] button, to display the main report composition window.

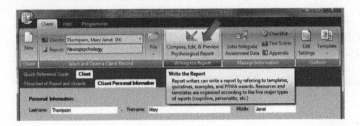

Write the Report

## Viewing the Main Report Composition Window

The Report Composition window will then be displayed, with the report template initialized with the identifying information for the new or selected client. You are now ready to start working on the report. Please note that a tour of the various sections and functions of this window is presented in the subsequent sections in this chapter. Much greater detail has been included in the User Manual, which is available through the [**Help**] commands throughout the program.

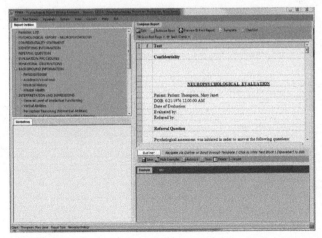

Main Report Composition Window

## Working on Report Content

As this is a new report, the client's name and date of birth will automatically be transferred to the template.

---

### NEUROPSYCHOLOGICAL EVALUATION

Patient: Thompson, Mary Janet
DOB: 6/21/1976 12:00:00 AM
Date of Evaluation:
Evaluated by:
Referred by:

---

Working on Content

---

Click inside the Template pane (the primary window pane in the upper right section of the window), then click into the large text box under the topic **Referral Question** to begin entering report information.

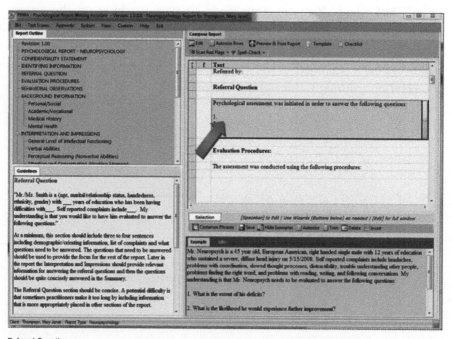

Referral Question

---

## Start Editing Mode

Whenever you navigate to, and then click into a section of the template to begin composing and editing, by pressing the **[Spaceband]**, you enter into **Edit Mode**, signified by the background of the text box displaying in a light yellow color:

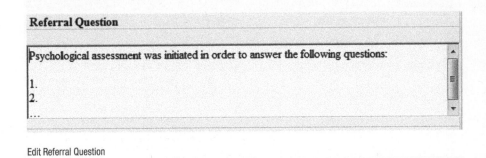

Edit Referral Question

## Viewing Guidelines and Example Text for the Report Topic

In the Guidelines pane in the bottom left portion of the window, you can view guidelines pertaining to the currently selected section of the report. Additionally, to help you compose the proper text for this topic, an example of good report content is presented in the Examples pane, at the bottom right of the window.

## Example of Using One of the PRWA Wizards

If you would like to see common phrases that are in standard use for this section for the type of psychological report you are composing, then click on the **[Common Phrases]** Wizard button, directly below the Template pane:

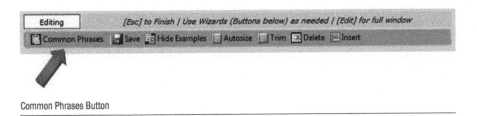

Common Phrases Button

## Selecting One or More Common Phrases

In the Common Phrases window, [√] check one or more phrases from the list on the right. You can edit the phrase in the bottom pane. When done, click on the [**Insert into text**] menu item in the top menu bar.

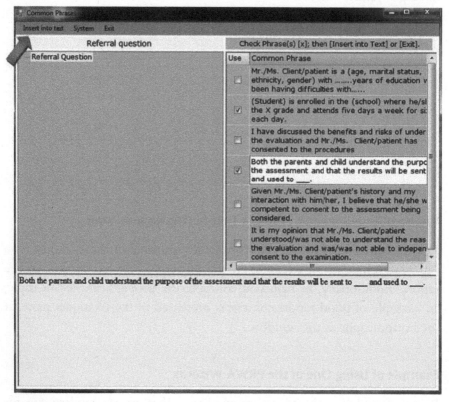

Common Phrases

The items selected will then be automatically inserted into the template, where your typing cursor was last positioned.

Referral Question Edit

## The PRWA Wizards

More detail for each of the Wizards is described in the User Manual. In particular, how to work with the integration of information, Systematic Treatment Selection, and the spell-check are detailed in the User Manual, and it should be noted that they are not described in the brief walk-through included in this chapter.

## Using the Outline/Navigation Pane for Quick Positioning

To quickly navigate to any major topic in the template, click on the desired heading in the Outline/Navigation pane, at the upper left of the window. For example, click on Medical History to directly access that portion of the template.

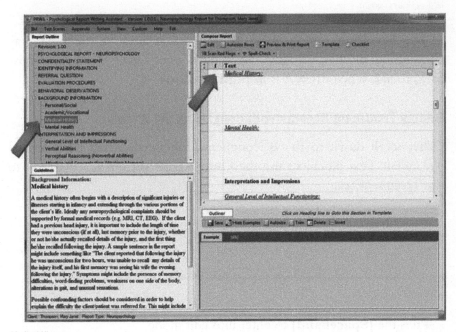

Medical History

PRWA will scroll the template to that heading.

To begin composing or editing text for that subject matter, click on the text box, and press the **[Spaceband]** to switch from **Scrolling** to **Editing Mode**.

> *Medical History:*
> The client's medical history prior to ...

Medical History Edit

When finished entering text, you can either click anywhere in the template outside of the text box or press the **[Escape]** key.

> *Medical History:*
> The client's medical history prior to the 5/15/2008 accident was generally unremarkable with the exception of having poor nutrition as an infant, some difficulties with coordination, and petit mal seizures. The seizures first occurred at age 18, were controlled with anticonvulsant medication, and, since age 30, she has neither had

Medical History Done

The **Scrolling** (or Viewing) **Mode** is indicated by the light gray background of the currently hightlighted text versus the light yellow background, when PRWA is in **Editing Mode**.

## Adding Treatment Recommendations Using the Wizard

Either scroll down to the Recommendations section and click on the Treatment Text block, or use the Outline pane for quick navigation to the Treatment text.

Treatment Recommendations

Press the **[Spaceband]** to enter into edit mode.

> *Treatment:*

Treatment Recommendations Edit

Click on **[Recommend]**.

Treatment Recommendations Button

The Recommendations Menu for Treatments will then be displayed.

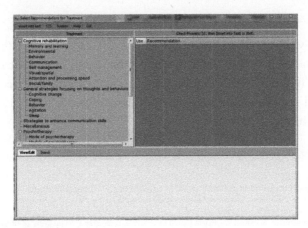

Treatment Recommendations Menu

In this example, we will select the subcategory Social/Family under Cognitive Rehabilitation Treatment Options and select two items for insertion into the report:

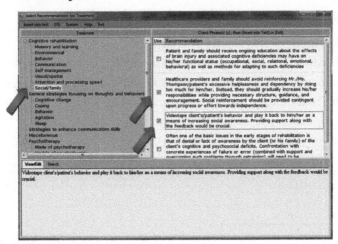

Treatment Recommendations Options

Click on the **[Insert into text]** menu item to insert the selected items into the report.

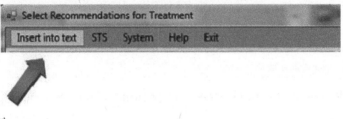

Insert into Text

As you will see, the inserted text has been entered into the report in the text block under the **Treatment** subheading. Note that recommendations do not need to be included for every category of recommendation. Avoid including too many recommendations (a total of six or less is usually all that are needed).

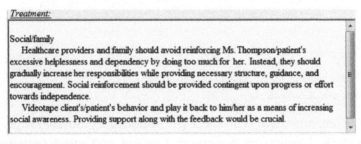

Treatment Recommendations Final

## Checking for Potentially Problematic ("Red Flag") Phrases

When the draft of the report is completed, click **Scan Red Flags** and this will search the document for potentially problematic phrases. The rationale for why these might be problematic along with suggestions for rephrasing will be displayed below the template.

Scan Red Flags

## Previewing, Copying, or Printing the Psychological Report

To see the fully composed and formatted report, click on the **[Preview & Print Template]** menu item in the Template menu bar, directly at the top of the Template window.

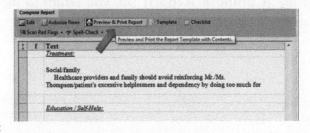

Preview and Print

## Viewing the Composed and Formatted Report

After Clicking on the **[Preview & Print Template]** menu item in the Template menu bar, PRWA changes focus to the **[Preview]** tab and displays the composed and formatted report. In our example, the following screenshot shows one screenfull from the fully formatted report.

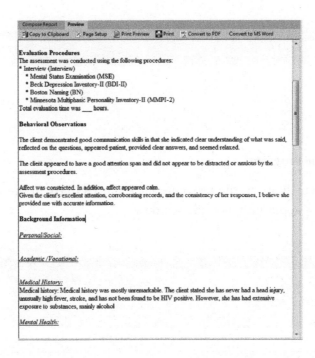

Preview Report

From here, you can select and then copy portions or all of the report or print the report.

### Returning to Report Composition

By Clicking the **[Compose Report]** tab, you return to the Template pane, and can continue viewing and editing your report.

Compose Report Button

### Finishing Your Work Session

Click on the Exit menu item in the Report Composition window main menu bar, to exit working on the template.

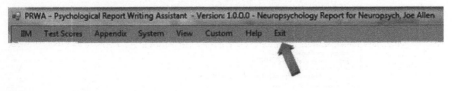

Exit

### Closing the Program

To end your work in the program, click the **[X]** box in the upper right of the main application console window.

Close Program

## Conclusion

This completes a basic walkthrough of the program. For a comprehensive reference guide to PRWA, please see the User Manual that is available through the **[Help]** commands throughout the software.

# Annotated Psychological Report

Mary Assessment, PhD, ABPP (Neuropsychology)
2984 Hospital Ave
Downtown, CA 23184

## CONFIDENTIAL PATIENT INFORMATION

Patient: Mr. Joe Neuropsych
Date of Birth: 1/1/65
Dates of Evaluation: 6/15/10 and 6/20/10
Evaluated by: Mary Assessment, PhD, ABPP (neuropsychology)
Referred by: Wilbur Jones, MD

## REFERRAL QUESTION

Mr. Neuropsych is a 45-year-old, European American, right-handed single male with 12 years of education who sustained a severe, diffuse head injury on 5/15/2008. Self-reported complaints include headaches, problems with coordination, slowed thought processes, distractibility, trouble understanding other people, problems finding the right word, and problems with reading, writing, and following conversations. My understanding is that you would like to have him evaluated to answer the following questions:

1. What is the nature and extent of his deficits?

Referral question includes demographic information, a listing of symptoms, and a listing of referral questions.

Core strategy 1 (numbering referral questions): The referral questions are numbered; later in the summary these questions are answered and organized according to the numbers that were originally used in the Referral Question section.

2. What is the likelihood he would experience further improvement?
3. Can he return to any form of employment?
4. What is the type and extent of care that would be required for him?

## EVALUATION PROCEDURES

> Assessment procedures are listed with the name of the test written out followed by its acronym.

Clinical interview, Wechsler Adult Intelligence Scale IV (WAIS-IV), Wechsler Memory Scale-IV (WMS-IV), Rey Auditory Verbal Learning Test (RAVLT), Bender Visual Motor Gestalt Test–II (Bender-II), Bender Memory, Aphasia Screening Test, Finger Tapping Test, Controlled Oral Word Association Test (COWAT), Trail Making, Beck Depression Inventory–II (BDI-II), Patient Competency Rating Form (Patient and Relative Forms), Millon Clinical Multiaxial Inventory–III (MCMI-III), Neuropsychological Symptom Checklist, Neuropsychological History Questionnaire, Sickness Impact Profile, and medical records by L. Chang, MD (7/15/2008), Frank Baum, MD (9/22/2008), and F. Fareley, MD (10/15/2009). Total evaluation time was 5 hours.

## BEHAVIORAL OBSERVATIONS

Mr. Neuropsych arrived on time to both his appointments and was oriented to person, place, time, and reason for the assessment. Although he needed to be driven to both assessment sessions by his father, he was able to walk to the consulting room unassisted. However, he limped and, as he walked, his head was shaking back and forth. On many occasions he struggled to pronounce words correctly. He often drifted from one subject to the next and required continual reminding to keep focused on a topic. In addition, he continually repeated the events of the accident even though he had previously provided the information. He also continually spoke of how frustrated he felt at being unable to do simple things that he felt he should be able to do without difficulty. His test performance was typically quite slow

> As much as possible the client's actual behavior is described with minimal use of interpretive statements.

and deliberate. For example, he took approximately 12 minutes to read and complete a self-report test having 21 items. Although there was a tendency to minimize some of his difficulties, particularly those related to psychosocial problems, he was generally cooperative and appeared to give his best effort to the tasks presented to him. Given the above observations combined with his test results, the results of the evaluation represent an accurate assessment of his current level of functioning.

A statement summarizing the validity of the assessment is provided at the end of the Behavioral Observations.

## BACKGROUND INFORMATION

### Personal/Social

Core strategy 2 (readability): Readability is enhanced by use of subheadings.

Mr. Neuropsych was a poor historian and, as a result, the following history was derived from a combination of an interview with his brother, medical records, and with some information provided by the patient. Mr. Neuropsych was born and raised in Ruraltown, California, and at age 20 moved to Midcity, California, where he has lived for the past 25 years. His parent's medical history was unremarkable. Mr. Neuropsych was married for 2 years between the ages of 28 and 30. At the time of his 5/15/2008 injury he was in a 5-year-long de facto relationship. Mr. Neuropsych's brother explained that the relationship did not survive the stress of the injury and subsequent hospital-

Clarification provided when necessary related to where the information came from.

ization. He does not have any contact with either of his previous partners. Mr. Neuropsych is currently living with various family members who take turns caring for him. His brother reported that Mr. Neuropsych is able to perform basic tasks around the property such as mowing the lawn, sweeping, and straightening up the house. However, he needs continual reminding even when doing simple, repetitive tasks. Mr. Neuropsych's brother also explained that Mr. Neuropsych is easily distracted, frequently misplaces things, and tires easily. Prior to the injury he used to enjoy fishing and working on his car. His only activities now are socializing with his family and attending a facility to assist persons with disabilities.

## Academic/Vocational

Information provided by Mr. Neuropsych's brother indicated that he had been an "average" student in school. He was evidently required to repeat fourth grade because he "had not grasped fundamental concepts." He did manage to complete high school although his grades in the past 2 years were mainly C's with some D's. Mr. Neuropsych has been employed doing various jobs such as driving trucks, cleaning houses, and mowing lawns. His most successful and long-term employment was between the ages of 38 and 42, when he worked as a plant operator. At the time of the accident he was employed cleaning offices.

## Medical

Medical history prior to the 5/15/2008 accident was generally unremarkable with the exception of having poor nutrition as an infant, and some difficulties with coordination. Mr. Neuropsych's brother stated that, prior to the 5/15/2008 injury, he had not had any previous head injuries, strokes, learning disabilities, substance abuse, tumors, unusually high fevers, or exposure to toxic materials.

> This information clarifies whether or not there might have been preexisting conditions that could explain the client's current difficulties.

On 5/15/2008 Mr. Neuropsych was a passenger in the front seat of a car that overturned, resulting in a severe head injury combined with numerous physical injuries. He was initially treated at MidCity Hospital from 5/15/2008 to 6/15/2008 and then transferred to MetroCity Rehabilitation Hospital from 6/15/2008 to 7/15/2008. The medical report by L. Chang, MD (7/15/2008) indicated that, upon intake to Metrocity Rehabilitation Hospital he scored only a 3 or 4 out of 15 on the Glasgow Coma Scale. He was unconscious for a total of 4 weeks. His first memory was seeing his father in his hospital room 6 weeks postinjury.

> The duration between the injury and the client's first memory is important to obtain, since it provides a general indication of the degree of post-traumatic complications that can be expected.

At discharge from Metrocity Rehabilitation Hospital it was noted that ". . . there were still indications of significant cognitive deficits involving his memory, insight, judgement, and intellectual functioning.

Emotionally there were still features of mood lability and occasional episodes of agitation" (p. 3).

## Mental Health

Mental health history prior to the 5/15/2008 injury was unremarkable. Currently he experiences mood swings approximately one to two times per week. These began approximately 3 months postinjury and are characterized by irritability, anger, a sense of hopelessness, difficulty with sleep onset and maintenance, and an exacerbation of the cognitive difficulties described previously.

> This information describes the onset, nature, frequency, and severity of the client's behavioral/emotional difficulties.

## IMPRESSIONS AND INTERPRETATIONS

### General Level of Intellectual Functioning

> Core strategy 2 (readability): Again, subheadings are used to enhance readability.

Overall level of intellectual functioning was in the Extremely Low range or the lower 1% of the population when compared with his age-related peers (Full Scale IQ = 62). There was little difference among his various scores, suggesting an overall lowering in his abilities. Given his history and pattern of test scores, I would estimate that his premorbid level of functioning would have been in the average to low average range or the lower 20% of the population.

### Verbal Abilities

> Core strategy 3 (use of functional domains): Interpretations are organized according to functional domains, rather than test by test.

Verbal abilities were in the Borderline to Extremely Low range or the 2nd percentile when compared with his age-related peers (Verbal Comprehension Index = 70). Despite these low scores, he can adequately comprehend spoken information, and he has an adequate fund of vocabulary words. However, he needs to absorb this information slowly, particularly if the information is even moderately complex.

> Core strategy 4 (minimal use of test scores): Although test scores are used, these are balanced by expanding what the scores mean by using

descriptions of abilities and (later) connecting the scores with behavioral observations). (This also illustrates core strategy 5 [integrate interpretations with all sources of data]).

Interpretations are expanded by not only describing the client's cognitive level and types of difficulties, but making the difficulty more easily understood by providing an example of a behavior illustrating it (qualitative description of behavioral observations).

Core strategy 5 (integration of interpretations): Interpretations are connected with additional sources of data as well as connected to the client's everyday world.

Core strategy 2 (readability) and core strategy 4 (minimize/clarify test-oriented language): Although test scores are used, they have been clarified by using everyday examples of how the client might have difficulties.

One particular difficulty is being able to come up with the correct word. For example, when given 60 seconds to come up with as many words as possible beginning with the letter "F," he was only able to come up with "fish" and "fox."

## Perceptual Reasoning

The patient's perceptual reasoning (nonverbal ability) was in the Borderline range or the 3rd percentile when compared with his age related peers (Perceptual Reasoning Index = 71). For example, he had difficulty assembling simple puzzles or reproducing basic designs. The designs he did draw were characterized by line tremor; overlapping, mild distortions; and drawing circles instead of dots. This test-related difficulty is consistent with the frustration he expressed when he was unable to drive a truck through three consecutive gates on his brother's farm. He stressed that it was a simple task and he knew that he should have been able to perform, but he felt he was unable to do so.

## Attention and Concentration

The patient's ability to attend to and concentrate on information was in the Extremely Low range or the 1st percentile when compared with his age-related peers (Working Memory Index = 63). This means that only one person in 100 would have scored this low. This also means he is moderately impaired in this area. For example, he was only able to repeat a maximum of four numbers that were read to him. His brother also noted that he needs to be constantly reminded in order to complete something. The above indicates he would have a difficult time paying attention during a conversation, recalling phone numbers, or doing two things at the same time.

> Core strategy 5 (integrate interpretations/connect to client's world): This sentence illustrates the implications the client's poor performance is likely to have in his everyday life.

## Processing Speed

The speed that Mr. Neuropsych can process information was in the Extremely Low range or the 1st percentile when compared with his age-related peers (Speed of Processing Index = 65). This suggests he would need extra time to learn new information or have difficulty quickly finding things in a room.

## Memory

Short-term memory was in the extremely low range or the .02 percentile when compared with his age-related peers (Immediate Memory Index = 56). This means that only 2 people in 1,000 would have scored this low. Thus, Mr. Neuropsych's memory and learning functions were similar to his other cognitive abilities, in that they were in the moderately to even severely impaired range. For example, he was unable to accurately reproduce from memory any of nine simple designs, even though he had worked with these designs for approximately 7 minutes. Even quite impaired persons can usually reproduce one or two designs from memory (and the average person will be able to reproduce four to five designs). Similarly, he could only recall 4 out of 15 simple words that were read to him. Even after practice trials his recall only increased to 5 out of the 15 words. In addition, his recall for words was easily interfered with by previous information he was required to work with.

> Core strategy 6 (connect interpretations to client's world/behavior): The behavioral observations help to anchor the expression of the client's poor memory into actual behaviors.

## Executive Functioning

History and behavioral observations indicate further difficulties in initiating, monitoring, sequencing, and having awareness over his behavior. As stated previously, Mr. Neuropsych needs continual reminding to stay focused on a task. Informal clinical assessment indicated that he has a difficult time sequencing fairly simple behaviors (alternating between fist-palm-back of hand). In many areas, Mr. Neuropsych minimized the impact of his injuries. For example, he felt that he himself could "do with ease" the following: remembering what he had for dinner the night before, staying involved in work activities, participating in group activities, and scheduling daily activities. In contrast, Mr. Neuropsych's brother rated each of these areas as Mr. Neuropsych being "unable" or "very difficult" for him to do. Thus he appears to have not only poor initiating and monitoring of his behavior, but his awareness of his deficits is quite poor.

## Personality

Review of personality suggests a general minimization or underreporting of psychological difficulties. For example, he endorsed items that indicated that he did not feel sad, depressed, angry, does not get any more tired than usual, and that he doesn't look any different than he did previously. I believe this is in part due to an optimistic outlook combined with a supportive, tolerant, patient family who are committed to taking care of him. Minimization of his difficulties is also due to little awareness of his deficits. Both minimization and poor awareness are adaptive in that they help to reduce the pain associated with fully attending to his difficulties. He also adapts by perceiving himself as being important and therefore more deserving of the care that is given to him. However, there were other indications that he has underlying but more hidden depression and anger.

## Client Strengths

Mr. Neuropsych has developed a reasonably good level of adjustment at least in part by minimizing, denying, and having poor awareness over his difficulties. In addition, he has a supportive, tolerant, patient family who are committed to caring for him. Under their direction he is able to contribute to family life by performing basic chores around the property such as mowing the lawn and feeding the pets. Additional strengths are that he has a reasonable fund of vocabulary words, understands basic information, and can recognize relevant from irrelevant details in his environment.

> Including client strengths helps to balance out the high emphasis on deficits that typically appears in reports. This can help with client morale. In addition, treatment planning might be developed in part by using these strengths.

## SUMMARY

Mr. Neuropsych is a 45-year-old, European American, right–handed, single male with 12 years of education who sustained a severe, diffuse head injury on 5/15/2008. His overall level of functioning is in the lower 1% of the population or the Extremely Low range. I would estimate his premorbid level of functioning was in the lower 20% of the population. His reading level is at the fourth-grade level, and he can spell and perform arithmetic at the fifth-grade levels. He has developed a reasonable level of emotional adjustment by minimizing his complaints, having poor awareness of their severity, and developing a sense that he should be attended to. An important client strength is that he is surrounded by a supportive, tolerant family who is committed to caring for him.

1. *Nature and extent of deficits:* Mr. Neuropsych is experiencing a wide range of moderate to severe deficits related to word finding, verbal fluency, spatial reasoning, reproduction of designs, coordination, attention, processing speed,

> Core strategy 1 (corresponding numbers): The numbers/content of questions used in the Referral Question section correspond with the numbers/content of the answers to these questions in the Summary.

short-term memory, and initiating, monitoring, and completing plans. While simple tasks such as dressing himself, mowing lawns, or checking on animals are within his capability, more complicated ones would be beyond his capability. For example, it would be unsafe for him to cook for himself since he would be likely to leave the burners on. Similarly, he would not be able to focus on financial tasks such as balancing a checkbook, paying bills, or responding to postal inquiries related to his finances. This is in contrast to his premorbid level of functioning when he could work independently, drive, take care of finances, care for himself, and become involved in marriage or marriage-type relationships. Any of the above would now be extremely difficult or impossible for him to manage.

2. *Likelihood he would experience further improvement:* Given the pattern and severity of his deficits, combined with the amount of time that has elapsed since his injury, I would not expect additional significant improvement. This is further complicated by his poor awareness of the extent of his deficits.

3. *Return to employment:* It is unlikely that he would be able to return to work other than within the context of a sheltered workshop with close supervision. However, his poor executive abilities suggest that even this may be problematic.

4. *Type and extent of care that would be required:* Given the extent and pattern of Mr. Neuropsych's deficits he would need extensive care. At the most he might be able to live in a carefully supervised home for disabled persons. His current situation with his family is ideal, in that they provide much of the day-to-day supervision for someone with his degree of impairment. However, this depends on their continued good will as well as their financial, physical, and emotional resources.

## RECOMMENDATIONS

Core strategy 6 (broad/relevant recommendations): recommendations are connected to the client's world and derived from the assessment results. They are also focused on the main issues the client is confronting, which in this case are optimizing his daily functioning and exploring the possibility of an additional placement.

1. Treatment should mainly consist of working with the family to optimize his living arrangements and should include:

   • Consult with family to determine what steps they might take to protect the patient from harming himself or others because of poor insight (e.g., locking up power tools and car keys).

   • Due to the patient's deficits in memory and organization, his environment should be highly structured. A regular schedule in which Mr. Neuropsych's chores are performed at the same time

every day can be helpful. The provision of a large and simple calendar, as well as a list of tasks to be accomplished, with a system for checking off each task as it is completed, may be useful in the home
- Organize communication to ensure understanding (remove environmental distractions, simplify instructions, repeat information, allow extra processing time).
- Compensate for attentional difficulties by breaking down complex tasks into simple ones, avoid multitasking, limit distractions (noise, television, music, people talking, other nearby activities).
- Confront with concrete experiences of failure or error combined with support and overcoming such problems through retraining.

2. Mr. Neuropsych and his family would benefit from learning about resources for brain injury survivors and their family (Brain Injury Association; www.biausa.org).

> Self-help resources are included as one of the recommendations.

3. The client should continue to be in a stable, supervised environment, which his family currently provides.
4. Consider placement in an adult day center program in order to provide stimulating recreational and social activities for him as well as some respite for the family.
5. Develop external reminders such as tying a string around Mr. Neuropsych's finger, posting a note, asking someone to remind the patient, using a tape recorder to record important information, using a chart that summarizes important information, as well as using checklists, medication organizers, medication alarms, cue cards, and/or Post-It notes.
6. Due to his poor problem-solving ability, forgetfulness, lack of appreciation for his problems and other cognitive problems, Mr. Neuropsych is not likely to exercise sound judgment in real life situations. As a result exploring the possibility of conservatorship is suggested.

Signature:
Name of examiner: Mary Assessment, PhD, ABPP (Neuropsychology)
Qualifications: Licensed psychologist (#0000), American Board of Professional Psychology (Neuropsychology)
Date:

# Checklist for General Psychological Report

The following checklist can be used to make sure that major components of the report have been included.

### Preliminary Information

❏ Indicate that report is confidential and cannot be released without author or client's permission.
❏ Include page numbering.
❏ Include identifying information (date of birth, gender, ethnicity, name of examiner, dates of examination).

### Referral Question

❏ Demographic/orienting *statement* (name, age, ethnicity, marital status, presenting issue/symptoms) as first sentence of referral question section.
❏ Include who has made the referral.
❏ Referral questions phrased as clear *questions* that can be answered and typically relate to *decisions* that need to be made.
❏ Referral questions are numbered (and then answered in the summary using corresponding numbers).

### Evaluation Procedures

❏ *Concise* listing of evaluation procedures.
❏ Evaluation procedures also lists records that were reviewed and interviews with corroborating sources.

### Behavioral Observations

❑ Behavioral observations include only ones that are relevant.
❑ Generally use concrete descriptions and not inferences.
❑ Statement of validity of assessment at end of behavioral observations.

### Background Information

❑ Identify who provided the information.
❑ History is in past tense (i.e., "The client reported . . .").
❑ History is brief, relevant, and focused but still in sufficient depth.
❑ History is in chronological order.
❑ History section is organized according to subheadings (personal/social, academic/vocational, etc.).
❑ Problem/symptoms include both the *nature* of the problems/symptoms as well as their onset, duration, frequency, and severity.

### Impressions and Interpretations

❑ Interpretation section uses subheadings and is organized according to domains (verbal abilities, coping style, interpersonal, etc.) and *not* presented test by test.
❑ Interpretations are integrated (results of multiple assessment combined, contradictory results taken into account).
❑ Interpretation section includes a minimum of numbers.
❑ Test results include standard (*t* scores, scaled scores) and *not* raw scores.
❑ Wechsler test results include index scores as well as FSIQ.
❑ IQ percentile equivalents and intelligence classifications are provided.
❑ Interpretation section uses everyday language (minimum of jargon/technical terms).
❑ Cognitive interpretations are explained in clear, nontechnical language.
❑ Wechsler subtests and scores are usually *not* mentioned/listed in interpretation section.

### Summary and Recommendations

❏ Summary section/paragraph *clearly* and *concisely* answers referral question(s) at the end of the summary and is numbered to correspond with the numbers listed for the referral questions in the referral question section.

❏ Recommendations do not overwhelm readers (generally six or less).

❏ Include most important recommendation(s) first.

❏ Include rationale for each recommendation (e.g., "In order to reduce Mr. Smith's anxiety it may be helpful to . . .").

❏ Recommendations are clear and specific (e.g., name/number of agency, names of books/web sites, focus of intervention).

❏ Signature, name, title, date included at end of report.

### General

❏ Avoid unprofessional phrases/terms (e.g., "a lot of," "got on well," "rehab," etc.).

❏ Translate jargon into everyday language.

❏ Use crisp, concise, professional style.

### Optional

❏ *Selective* direct client quotes in history (and/or behavioral observations).

❏ Everyday examples of cognitive interpretations are given.

❏ Significant discrepancies within cognitive test results are noted (between indexes).

❏ Include content of selected items (but not items themselves), client quotes, and behavioral observations to illustrate the quality of responses.

❏ Vocational interpretations clearly compare and contrast the participant's abilities/personality with the requirements of his/her current/desired occupation (and are organized around relevant domains; cognitive strengths/weaknesses, personality, interpersonal style, social demands, etc.).

❏ DSM-5 diagnosis included if necessary.

# Checklist for Forensic Psychological Report

The following checklist can be used to make sure that major components of a forensic report have been included.

## Preliminary Information

❑ Indicate relative confidentiality and the extent to which the report can be released without the author's or client's permission.

❑ Include page numbering.

❑ Include identifying information (date of birth, gender, ethnicity, name of examiner, dates of examination).

## Referral Question

❑ Demographic/orienting *statement* (name, age, ethnicity, marital status, presenting issue/symptoms) as first sentence of referral question section.

❑ Include who has made the referral.

❑ Forensic referral questions stated *clearly* and typically relate to *decisions* that need to be made regarding the defendant/plaintiff.

❑ Referral questions are numbered (and then answered in the summary using corresponding numbers).

## Evaluation Procedures

❑ *Concise* listing of evaluation procedures.

❑ Evaluation procedures also lists records that were reviewed and interviews with corroborating sources.

### Behavioral Observations

❏ Behavioral observations include only ones that are relevant.
❏ Generally use concrete descriptions and not inferences.
❏ Statement of validity of assessment at end of behavioral observations.

### Background Information

❏ Identify who provided the information.
❏ History is in past tense (i.e., "The client reported . . .").
❏ History is brief, relevant, and focused but still in sufficient depth.
❏ History is in chronological order.
❏ History section is organized according to subheadings (personal/ social, legal, academic/vocational, etc.).
❏ Problem/symptoms include both the *nature* of the problems/symptoms as well as their onset, duration, frequency, and severity.

### Findings (Impressions and Interpretations)

❏ Data are included only if relevant to the forensic questions being asked.
❏ Include multiple and converging sources of information/data if possible.
❏ Observations are clearly differentiated from inferences.
❏ Findings section uses subheadings and is organized according to domains (verbal abilities, coping style, interpersonal, etc.) and *not* presented test by test.
❏ Interpretations are integrated (results of multiple assessment combined, contradictory results taken into account).
❏ Interpretation section includes a minimum of numbers.
❏ Test results include standard (t scores, scaled scores) and *not* raw scores.
❏ Wechsler test results include index scores as well as FSIQ.
❏ IQ percentile equivalents and intelligence classifications are provided.
❏ Interpretation section uses everyday language (minimum of jargon/technical terms).
❏ Cognitive interpretations are explained in clear, nontechnical language.
❏ Wechsler subtests and scores are usually *not* mentioned/listed in interpretation section.

### Summary and Recommendations

❑ Summary section clearly answers the referral questions.

❑ Answers to referral questions (opinions) are numbered, and the numbers correspond to the questions listed in the referral question section.

❑ Opinions are always supported by data.

❑ Links between information/data and opinions are clarified (e.g., Given X, Y, and Z, Mr. Smith is unlikely to be competent to stand trial . . .").

❑ Alternative conclusions are considered.

❑ Recommendations (if included) do not overwhelm readers (generally six or less).

❑ Include most important recommendation(s) first.

❑ Include rationale for each recommendation (e.g. "In order to reduce Mr. Smith's anxiety it may be helpful to . . .").

❑ Recommendations are clear and specific (i.e., name/number of agency, names of books/web sites, focus of intervention).

❑ Signature, name, title, date included at end of report.

### General

❑ Avoid unprofessional phrases/terms (e.g., "a lot of," "got on well," "rehab," etc.).

❑ Translate jargon into everyday language.

❑ Use crisp, concise, professional style.

### Optional

❑ *Selective* direct client quotes in history (and/or behavioral observations).

❑ Everyday examples of cognitive interpretations are given.

❑ Significant discrepancies within cognitive test results are noted (between indexes).

❑ *DSM-5* diagnosis included if necessary.

# Selected Resources for Psychological Report Writing

## BOOKS ON REPORT WRITING

Ackerman, M. J. (2006). *Clinician's guide to child custody evaluations* (3rd ed.). Hoboken, NJ: Wiley.

Allyn, J. B. (2012). *Writing to clients and referring professionals about psychological assessment results: A handbook of style and grammar.* New York, NY: Routledge.

Armengol, C. G., Kaplan, E., & Moes, E. J. (Eds.). (2001). *The consumer-oriented neuropsychological report.* Lutz, FL: Psychological Assessment Resources.

Braaten, E. B. (2007). *The child clinician's report writing handbook.* New York, NY: Guilford Press.

Bradley-Johnson, S., & Johnson, C. M. (2006). *A handbook for writing effective psychoeducational reports.* (2nd ed.). Austin, TX: PRO-ED.

Goldfinger, K., & Pomerantz, A. M. (2010). *Psychological assessment and report writing.* Thousand Oaks, CA: Sage.

Greenfield, D. P., & Gottschalk, J. A. (2009). *Writing forensic reports: A guide for mental health professionals.* New York, NY: Springer.

Lichtenberger, E. O., Mather, N., Kaufman, N. L., & Kaufman, A. S. (2004). *Essentials of assessment report writing.* Hoboken, NJ: Wiley.

Zuckerman, E. L. (2005). *The clinician's thesaurus three: A guidebook for wording psychological reports* (6th ed.). New York, NY: Guilford Press.

## BOOKS WITH SAMPLE REPORTS

Groth-Marnat, G. (2009a). *Handbook of psychological assessment* (5th ed.). Hoboken, NJ: Wiley.

Greenfield, D. P., & Gottschalk, J. A. (2009). *Writing forensic reports: A guide for mental health professionals.* New York, NY: Springer.

Harwood, T. M. H., Beutler, L. E., & Groth-Marnat, G. (2011). *Integrative assessment of adult personality* (3rd ed.). New York, NY: Guilford Press.

Heilbrun, K., Marczyk, G. G., & Dematteo, D. (2002). *Forensic mental health assessment: A casebook.* New York, NY: Oxford University Press.

Lowman, R. L. (1991). *The clinical practice of career assessment: Interests, abilities, personality* (2nd ed.). Washington, DC: American Psychological Association.

Morgan, J. E., Baron, I. S., & Ricker, J. H. (Eds.). (2010). *Casebook of clinical neuropsychology.* New York, NY: Oxford University Press.

## Articles

American Psychological Association (1994). Guidelines for child custody evaluations in divorce proceedings. *American Psychologist, 49,* 677–680.

American Psychological Association Committee on Professional Practice and Standards. (1998). *Guidelines for psychological evaluations in child protection matters.* Washington, DC: American Psychological Association.

Brenner, E. (2003). Consumer-focused psychological assessment. *Professional Psychology: Research and Practice, 34,* 240–247.

Grisso, T. (2010). Guidance for improving forensic reports: A review of common errors. *Open Access Journal of Forensic Psychology, 2,* 102–115; www.forensicpsychol ogyunbound.ws/-2010.2:233-240

Groth-Marnat, G. (2009b). The five assessment issues you meet when you go to heaven. *Journal of Personality Assessment, 91,* 303–310.

Groth-Marnat, G., & Horvath, L. S. (2006). The psychological report: A review of current controversies. *Journal of Clinical Psychology, 62,* 73–81.

Harvey, V. S. (1997). Improving readability of psychological reports. *Professional Psychology: Research and Practice, 28,* 271–274.

Harvey, V. S. (2006). Variables affecting the clarity of reports. *Journal of Clinical Psychology, 62,* 5–18.

Pelco, L. E., Ward, S. B., Coleman, L., & Young, J. (2009). Teacher ratings of three psychological report styles. *Training and Education in Professional Psychology, 3* (1), 19–27.

Pieniadz, J., & Kelland, D. Z. (2001). Reporting scores in neuropsychological assessment: Ethical, validity, practicality, and more. In C. G. Armengol, E. Kaplan, & E. J. Moes (Eds.), *The consumer-oriented neuropsychological report* (pp. 123–140). Lutz, FL: Psychological Assessment Resources.

Witt, P. H. (2010). Forensic report checklist. *Open Access Journal of Forensic Psychology, 2,* 233–240. http://forensicpsychologyunbound.ws/-2010.2:233-240

## Internet Links With Sample Reports

Discussion of controversy of Mike Tyson report and links to actual report: http://mentalhealth.about.com/cs/academicpsychology/a/tyson_2.htm

DVD with analysis of Jeffrey Dahmer case: www.caldwellreport.com/publications.aspx

Neuropsychoogical and psychoeducational reports and report writing software: www.thepsycwriter.com/index.html

Psychological report of Unabomber/Ted Kaczynski: www.paulcooijmans.com/
psychology/unabombreport.html

## TREATMENT PLANNING

Beutler, L. E., Clarkin, I. F., & Bongar, B. (2000). *Guidelines for the systematic treatment of the depressed patient.* New York, NY: Oxford University Press.

Jongsma, A. E., & Peterson. L. M. (2006). *The complete adult psychotherapy treatment planner* (4th ed.). Hoboken, NJ: Wiley.

Jongsma, A. E., Peterson, L. M. & McInnis, W. P. (2006). *The child psychotherapy treatment planner* (4th ed.). Hoboken, NJ: Wiley.

Lemsky, C. M. (2000). Neuropsychological assessment and treatment planning. In G. Groth-Marnat (Eds.), *Neuropsychological assessment in clinical practice: A guide to test interpretation and integration* (pp. 535–574). Hoboken, NJ: Wiley.

Nathan, P. E., & Gorman, J. M. (2007). *A guide to treatments that work* (3rd ed.). New York, NY: Oxford University Press.

Scherer, M. (2011). *Assistive technologies and other supports for people with brain impairment.* New York, NY: Springer.

## BEST PRACTICES/EVIDENCE-BASED TREATMENTS FOR TREATMENT PLANNING

American Psychiatric Association: www.psychiatryonline.com/pracGuide/
pracGuideTopic_9.aspx

American Psychological Association: www.apa.org/practice/prof.html

Society of Clinical Psychology: www.psychologicaltreatments.org

PracticeWise Evidence-Based Services [PWEBS]: www.practicewise
.com

## SELF-HELP RESOURCES

Norcross, J. C. (2006). Integrating self-help into psychotherapy: 16 practical suggestions. *Professional Psychology: Research & Practice, 37*, 683–693.

Norcross, J., Santrock, J. W., Campbell, L. F., Smith, T. P., Sommer, R., & Zuckerman, E. L. (2012). *Authoritative guide to self-help resources in mental health* (4th ed.). New York, NY: Guilford Press.

# References

Ackerman, M. J. (2006). *Clinician's guide to child custody evaluations* (3rd ed.). Hoboken, NJ: Wiley.

Acklin, M. W., McDowell, C. J., Verschell, M. S., & Chan, D. (2000). Interobserver agreement, intraobserver reliability, and the Rorschach Comprehensive System. *Journal of Personality Assessment, 74*, 15–47.

Allyn, J. B. (2012). *Writing to clients and referring professionals about psychological assessment results: A handbook of style and grammar.* New York, NY: Routledge.

American Psychological Association. (1994). Guidelines for child custody evaluations in divorce proceedings. *American Psychologist, 49*, 677–680.

American Psychological Association. (2012a). Guidelines for the evaluation of dementia and age-related cognitive decline. *American Psychologist, 67*(1), 1–9.

American Psychological Association. (2012b). Guidelines for psychological practice with lesbian, gay, and bisexual clients. *American Psychologist, 67*(1), 10–42.

American Psychological Association. (2012c). Guidelines for assessment and intervention with persons with disabilities. *American Psychologist, 67*(1), 43–62.

American Psychological Association (2013). Specialty guidelines for forensic psychology. *American Psychologist, 68*(1), 7–19.

American Psychological Association Committee on Professional Practice and Standards. (1998). *Guidelines for psychological evaluations in child protection matters.* Washington, DC: American Psychological Association.

American Psychological Association Committee on Professional Practice and Standards. (2002). Ethical principles of psychologists and code of conduct. *American Psychologist, 57*, 1060–1075.

APA Task Force on Evidence-Based Practice. (2006). Evidence-based practice in psychology. *American Psychologist, 61*, 271–285.

Archer, R. P. (2006). *Forensic uses of clinical assessment instruments.* Mahwah, NJ: Erlbaum.

Archer, R. P., Buffington-Vollum, J. K., Stredny, R. V., & Handel, R. W. (2006). A survey of test use patterns among forensic psychologists. *Journal of Personality Assessment, 87*, 64–94. doi: 10.1207/s15327752jpa8701_07

Armengol, C. G. (2001). The referral process. In C. G. Armengol, E. Kaplan, & E. J. Moes (Eds.), *The consumer-oriented neuropsychological report* (pp. 47–60). Lutz, FL: Psychological Assessment Resources.

Armengol, C. G., Kaplan, E. & Moes, E. J. (Eds.). (2001). *The consumer-oriented neuro-psychological report*. Lutz, FL: Psychological Assessment Resources.

Barlow, D. (2008). *Clinical handbook of psychological disorders*. New York, NY: Guilford Press.

Barlow, D. H. (2004). Psychological treatments. *American Psychologist, 59*, 869–878.

Beutler, L. E. (2009). Making science matter in clinical practice: Redefining psycho-therapy. *Clinical Psychology: Science & Practice, 17*, 301–317.

Beutler, L. E., Clarkin, I. F., & Bongar, B. (2000). *Guidelines for the systematic treatment of the depressed patient*. New York, NY: Oxford University Press.

Beutler, L. E., & Groth-Marnat, G. (2003). *Integrative assessment of adult personality*. New York, NY: Guilford Press.

Beutler, L. E., Harwood, T. M., Kimpara, S., Verdirame, D., & Blau, K. (2011). Coping style. *Journal of Clinical Psychology, 67*, 176–183. doi: 10.1002/jclp.20752

Beutler, L. E., Harwood, T. M., Michelson, A., Song, X., & Holman, J. (2011). Resistance/reactance level. *Journal of Clinical Psychology, 67*, 133–142. doi: 10.1002/jclp.20753

Beutler, L. E., & Malik, M. (Eds.). (2002). *Rethinking the DSM: A psychological perspec-tive*. Washington, DC: American Psychological Association.

Beutler, L. E., Moleiro, C., & Talebi, H. (2002). Resistance. In J. C. Norcross (Ed.), *Psychotherapy relationships that work: Therapist contributions and responsiveness to patient's needs* (pp. 129–444). New York, NY: Oxford University Press.

Blais, M. A., & Smith, S. R. (2008). Improving the integrative process in psychologi-cal assessment: Data organizing and report writing. In R. P. Archer & S. R. Smith (Eds.), *Personality assessment* (pp. 405–440). New York, NY: Routledge.

Bow, J. N. and Quinnell, F. A. (2002). *A critical review of child custody evaluation reports*. *Family Court Review, 40,* 164–176.

Braaten, E. B. (2007). *The child clinician's report writing handbook*. New York, NY: Guilford Press.

Bradley-Johnson, S., & Johnson, C. M. (2006). *A handbook for writing effective psycho-educational reports* (2nd ed.). Austin, TX: Pro-Ed.

Brenner, E. (2003). Consumer-focused psychological assessment. *Professional Psychology: Research and Practice, 34*, 240–247.

Buchanan, A., Binder, R., Norko, M., Swartz, M. (2012). Resource document on psychiatric violence risk assessment. *American Journal of Psychiatry, 169*(3), 1–10.

Budd, K. S., Clark, J., & Connell, M. A. (2011). *Evaluation of parenting capacity in child protection*. New York, NY: Oxford University Press.

Butcher, J. N., Perry, J. N., & Atlis, M. M. (2000). Validity and utility of computer-based test interpretation. *Psychological Assessment, 12*, 6–18.

Christy, A., Douglas, K., Otto, R., & Petrila, J. (2004). Juveniles evaluated incompetent to proceed: Characteristics and quality of mental health professionals' evaluations. *Professional Psychology: Research and Practice, 35*(4), 380–388. doi: 10.1037/0735-7028.35.4.380

Das, J. P., & Naglieri, J. A. (1994). *Das-Naglieri Cognitive Assessment System: Standardization Test Battery*. Chicago, IL: Riverside Press.

Den Boer, P. C. A. M., Wiersma, D., & Van Den Bosch, R. J. (2004). Why is self help neglected in the treatment of emotional disorders? A meta-analysis. *Psychological Medicine, 34,* 959–971.

Edinger, J. D., & Carney, C. E. (2008). *Overcoming insomnia.* New York, NY: Oxford University Press.

Finn, S. E. (2007). *In our client's shoes: Theory and techniques of therapeutic assessment.* Mahwah, NJ: Erlbaum.

Finn, S. E. (2012). *Therapeutic assessment: Using psychological testing to help clients change.* New York, NY: Routledge.

Finn, S. E., Fischer, C. T., & Handler, L. (2012). *Collaborative/therapeutic assessment: A casebook and guide.* Hoboken, NJ: Wiley.

Finn, S. E., Moes, E. J., & Kaplan, E. (2001). The consumer's point of view. In C. G. Armengol, E. Kaplan, & E. J. Moes (Eds.), *The consumer-oriented neuropsychological report* (pp. 13–46). Lutz, FL: Psychological Assessment Resources.

Fischer, C. (2012). *Individualizing psychological assessment* (2nd ed.). Hillsdale, NJ: Erlbaum.

Foa, E. B., Hembree, E. A., & Rothbaum, B. O. (2007). *Prolonged exposure therapy for PTSD: Emotional processing of traumatic experiences.* New York, NY: Oxford University Press.

Foa, E. B., Yadin, E. & Lichner, T. K. (2012). *Exposure and response (ritual) prevention prevention for obsessive-compulsive disorder: A cognitive-behavioral program.* (2nd ed.). New York, NY: Oxford University Press

Gannellen, R. J. (2007). Assessing normal and abnormal personality functioning: Strengths and weaknesses of self report, observer, and performance-based methods. *Journal of Personality Assessment, 89,* 30–40.

Geffken, G. R., Keeley, M. L., Kellison, I., Storch, E. A., & Rodrigue, J. R. (2006). Parental adherence to child psychologist's recommendations from psychological testing. *Professional Psychology: Research and Practice, 37,* 499–505. doi: 10.1037/0735-7028.37.5.499

Goldfinger, K., & Pomerantz, A. M. (2010). *Psychological assessment and report writing.* Thousand Oaks, CA: Sage.

Greenfield, D. P., & Gottschalk, J. A. (2009). *Writing forensic reports: A guide for mental health professionals.* New York, NY: Springer.

Grisso, T. (2010). Guidance for improving forensic reports: A review of common errors. *Open Access Journal of Forensic Psychology, 2,* 102–115. www.forensicpsychologyunbound.ws/-2010.2:233-240

Groth-Marnat, G. (2000). Visions of clinical assessment: Then, now, and a brief history of the future. *Journal of Clinical Psychology, 56,* 349–365.

Groth-Marnat, G. (2009a). *Handbook of psychological assessment* (5th ed.). Hoboken, NJ: Wiley.

Groth-Marnat, G. (2009b). The five assessment issues you meet when you go to heaven. *Journal of Personality Assessment, 91,* 303–310.

Groth-Marnat, G., & Horvath, L. S. (2006). The psychological report: A review of current controversies. *Journal of Clinical Psychology, 62*(1), 73–81. doi: 10.1002/jclp20201

Groth-Marnat, G., Roberts, R., & Beutler, L. E. (2001). Client characteristics and psychotherapy: Perspectives, support, interactions, and implications. *Australian Psychologist, 36*, 115–121.

Harvey, V. S. (1997). Improving readability of psychological reports. *Professional Psychology: Research and Practice, 28*, 271–274.

Harvey, V. S. (2006). Variables affecting the clarity of reports. *Journal of Clinical Psychology, 62*(1), 5–18. doi: 10.1002/jclp.20196

Harwood, T. M., Beutler, L. E., & Groth-Marnat, G. (2011). *Integrative assessment of adult personality.* (3rd ed.). New York, NY: Guilford Press.

Heilbrun, K. (2009). *Evaluation for risk of violence in adults.* New York, NY: Oxford University Press.

Heilbrun, K., & Collins, S. (1995). Evaluations of trial competency and mental state at the time of offense: Report characteristics. *Professional Psychology: Research and Practice, 26*, 61–67.

Heilbrun, K., Grisso, T., & Goldstein, A. (2008). *Foundations of forensic mental health assessment.* New York, NY: Oxford University Press.

Heilbrun, K., Marczyk, G. G., & Dematteo, D. (2002). *Forensic mental health assessment: A casebook.* New York, NY: Oxford University Press.

Houts, A. C. (2002). Discovery, invention, and the expansion of the modern *Diagnostic and Statistical Manuals of Mental Disorders.* In L. E. Beutler & M. L. Malik (Eds.), *Rethinking the DSM: A psychological perspective* (pp. 17–69). Washington, DC: American Psychological Association.

Jongsma, A. E., & Peterson. L. M. (2006). *The complete adult psychotherapy treatment planner* (4th ed.). Hoboken, NJ: Wiley.

Jongsma, A. E., Peterson, L. M., & McInnis, W. P. (2006). *The child psychotherapy treatment planner* (4th ed.). Hoboken, NJ: Wiley.

Kvaal, S., Choca, J., Groth-Marnat, G., & Davis, A. (2011). The Integrated psychological report. In T. M. Harwood, L. E. Beutler, & G. Groth-Marnat (Eds.), *Integrative assessment of adult personality* (3rd ed.). (pp. 413-446). New York, NY: Guilford Press.

Lemsky, C. M. (2000). Neuropsychological assessment and treatment planning. In G. Groth-Marnat (Eds.), *Neuropsychological assessment in clinical practice: A guide to test interpretation and integration* (pp. 535–574). Hoboken, NJ: Wiley.

Levak, R. W., Hogan, S., Beutler, L. E., & Song, X. (2011). Integrating and applying assessment information: Decision making, patient feedback, and consultation. In T. M. Harwood, L. E. Beutler, & G. Groth-Marnat (Eds.), *Integrative assessment of adult personality* (3rd ed.). (pp. 373–412). New York, NY: Guilford Press.

Levak, R. W., Marks, P. A., & Nelson, G. E. (1990). *Therapist guide to the MMPI and MMPI-2.* Muncie, IN: Acclerated Development.

Levak, R. W., Siegel, L., Nichols, D., & Stolberg, R. (2011). *Therapeutic feedback with the MMPI-2: A positive psychology approach.* New York, NY: Routledge.

Lezak, M. D., Howieson, D. B., Bigler, E. D., & Tranel, D. (2012). *Neuropsychological assessment* (5th ed.). New York, NY: Oxford University Press.

Lichtenberger, E. O. (2006). Computer utilization and clinical judgment in psychological assessment reports. *Journal of Clinical Psychology, 62*, 19–32. doi: 10.1002/jclp.2019

Lichtenberger, E. O., Mather, N., Kaufman, N. L., & Kaufman, A. S., (2004). *Essentials of psychological report writing*. Hoboken, NJ: Wiley.

Loeb, A. A. (1996). *Independent living scales*. San Antonio, TX: Pearson Assessment.

Lowman, R. L. (1991). *The clinical practice of career assessment: Interests, abilities, personality*. Washington, DC: American Psychological Association.

Luria, A. R. (1973). *The working brain*. New York, NY: Basic Books.

Lynn, S. J., & Shindler, K. (2002). The role of hypnotizability assessment in treatment. *American Journal of Clinical Hypnosis, 44*, 185–197.

Marks, I. M., Cavanagh, K., & Gega, L. (2007). *Hands-on help: Computer-aided psychotherapy*. London, England: Psychology Press.

McMinn, M. R., Buchanan, T., Ellens, B. M., & Ryan, M. K. (1999). Technology, professional practice, and ethics: Survey findings, and implications. *Professional Psychology: Research and Practice, 30*, 165–172.

McMinn, M. R., Ellens, B. M., & Soref, E. (1999). Ethical perspectives and practice behaviors involving computer-based test interpretation. *Professional Psychology: Research and Practice, 30*, 71–77.

Meyer, G. J., Viglione, D. J., Mihura, J. L., Erard, R. E., & Erdberg, P. (2011). Rorschach Performance Assessment System: Administration, coding, interpretation, and technical manual. Toledo, OH: Rorschach Performance Assessment System.

Michaels, M. H. (2006). Ethical considerations in writing psychological reports. *Journal of Clinical Psychology, 62*(1), 47–58. doi: 10.1002/jclp.20199

Miller, H. (2001). *M-FAST: Miller Forensic Assessment of Symptoms Test professional manual*. Lutz, FL: Psychological Assessment Resources.

Morgan, J. E., Baron, I. S., & Ricker, J. H. (Eds.). (2010). *Casebook of clinical neuropsychology*. New York, NY: Oxford University Press.

Munsinger, H. L., & Karlson, K. W. (1994). *Uniform child custody evaluation system*. Odessa, FL: Psychological Assessment Resources.

Nathan, P. E., & Gorman, J. M. (2007). *A guide to treatments that work* (3rd ed.). New York, NY: Oxford University Press.

Nock, M. K., & Kazdin, A. E. (2005). Randomized control trial of a brief intervention for increasing participation in parent management training. *Journal of Consulting and Clinical Psychology, 73*, 872–879.

Norcross, J. C. (2006). Integrating self-help into psychotherapy: 16 practical suggestions. *Professional Psychology: Research & Practice, 37*, 683–693.

Norcross, J. C. (Ed.). (2011). *Psychotherapy relationships that work* (2nd ed.). New York, NY: Oxford University Press.

Norcross, J., & Lambert, M. J. (2011). Psychotherapy relationships that work II. *Psychotherapy, 48*(1), 4–8. doi: 10.1037/a0022180

Norcross, J., Santrock, J. W., Campbell, L. F., Smith, T. P., Sommer, R., & Zuckerman, E. L. (2012). *Authoritative guide to self-help resources in mental health* (4th ed.). New York, NY: Guilford Press.

O'Hanlon, B., & Bertolino, B. (2012). *The therapist's notebook on positive psychology: Activities, exercises, and handouts*. New York, NY: Routledge.

Otis, J. D. (2007). *Managing chronic pain*. New York, NY: Oxford University Press.

Otto, R. K., & Heilbrun, K. (2002). The practice of forensic psychology: A look toward the future in light of the past. *American Psychologist, 57*, 5–10.

Packer, I. K. (2009). *Evaluation of criminal responsibility.* New York, NY: Oxford University Press.

Pelco, L. E., Ward, S. B., Coleman, L., & Young, J. (2009). Teacher ratings of three psychological report styles. *Training and Education in Professional Psychology, 3*(1), 19–27.

Pieniadz, J., & Kelland, D. Z. (2001). Reporting scores in neuropsychological assessment: Ethical, validity, practicality, and more. In C. G. Armengol, E. Kaplan, & E. J. Moes (Eds.), *The consumer-oriented neuropsychological report* (pp. 123–140). Lutz, FL: Psychological Assessment Resources.

Poythress, N., Nicholson, R., Otto, R. K., Edens, J. F., Bonnie, R. J., Monahan, J., & Hoge, S. K. (1999). *The MacArthur Competence Assessment Tool–Criminal Adjudication: Professional manual.* Odessa, FL: Psychological Assessment Resources.

Rogers, R., Tillbrook, C. E., & Sewell, K. W. (2004). *Evaluation of competence to stand trial–Revised: Professional manual.* Odessa, FL: Psychological Assessment Resources.

Rusin, M. J., & Jongsma, A. E. (2001). *The rehabilitation psychology treatment planner.* New York, NY: Wiley.

Sattler, J. M. (2008). *Assessment of children: Cognitive functions* (5th ed.). San Diego, CA: Author.

Scherer, M. (2011). *Assistive technologies and other supports for people with brain impairment.* New York, NY: Springer.

Schmidt, F. L., & Hunter, J. E. (1998). The validity and utility of selection methods in personnel psychology: Practical and theoretical implications of 85 years of research findings. *Psychological Bulletin, 124*, 262–274.

Schmidt, F. L., & Hunter, J. E. (2004). General mental ability in the work place. *Journal of Personality and Social Psychology, 86*, 162–173.

Shectman, F. (1979). Problems in communicating psychological understanding: Why won't they listen to me? *American Psychologist, 34*, 781–790.

Shedler, J. (2010). The efficacy of psychodynamic psychotherapy. *American Psychologist, 65*, 98–109.

Shin, H. B., & Kominski, R. A. (2010). Language use in the United States: 2007. Retrieved from www.census.gov/population/www/socdemo/language/ACS-12.pdf

Smith, T. B., Rodriguez, M. A., & Bernal, G. (2011). Culture. *Journal of Clinical Psychology: In Session, 67*, 166–175. doi: 10.1002/jclp.20757

Snyder, C. R., Lopez, S., & Pedrotti, J. (2011). *Positive psychology: The scientific and practical explorations of human strengths* (2nd ed.). Thousand Oaks, CA: Sage.

Snyder, C. R., Ritschel, L. A., Rand, K. L., & Berg, C. J. (2006). Balancing psychological assessments: Including strengths and home in client reports. *Journal of Clinical Psychology, 62*, 33–46.

Sommers-Flanagan, R., & Sommers-Flanagan, J. (2009). *Clinical interviewing* (4th ed.). Hoboken, NJ: Wiley.

Sparrow, S. S., Cicchetti, D. V., & Balla, D. A., (2005). *Vineland Adaptive Behavior Scales* (2nd ed.). Circle Pines, MN: American Guidance Service.

Strauss, E., Sherman, E. M. S., & Spreen, O. (2006). *A compendium of neuropsychological tests: Administration, norms, and commentary* (3rd ed.). New York, NY: Oxford University Press.

Sturmey, P., & Hersen, M. (2012). *Handbook of evidence-based practice in clinical psychology* (Vols. I and II). Hoboken, NJ: Wiley.

Tallent, N. (1993). *Psychological report writing* (4th ed.). Englewood Cliffs, NJ: Prentice Hall.

Tombaugh, T. N. (1996). *The test of memory malingering.* Los Angeles, CA: Western Psychological Services.

United States Census Bureau News. (2007, May 17). *Minority population tops 100 million.* Washington, DC: U.S. Department of Commerce.

Wampold, B. E. (2001). *The great psychotherapy debate: Model, methods, and findings.* Mahwah, NJ: Erlbaum.

Wampold, B. E. (2010). *The basics of psychotherapy: An introduction to theory and practice.* Washington DC: American Psychological Association.

Webster, C., Douglas, K., Eaves, D., & Hart, S. (1997). *HCR-20: Assessing risk for violence* (version 2). Vancouver, BC, Canada: Simon Fraser University.

WHO World Mental Health Survey Consortium. (2004). Prevalence, severity, and unmet need for treatment of mental disorders in the World Health Organization world mental health surveys. *Journal of the American Medical Association, 291,* 2581–2590.

Witt, P. H. (2009). *Evaluation of sexually violent predators.* New York, NY: Oxford University Press.

Witt, P. H. (2010). Forensic report checklist. *Open Access Journal of Forensic Psychology, 2,* 233–240; http://forensicpsychologyunbound.ws/-2010.2:233-240

Worthen, M. D., & Moering, R. G. (2012). A practical guide to conducting VA compensation and pension exams for PTSD and other mental disorders. *Psychological Injury and the Law, 4*(3–4), 1-30. doi: 10.1007/s12207-011-9115-2

Wright, A. J. (2011). *Conducting psychological assessment: A guide for practitioners.* Hoboken, NJ: Wiley.

Zapf, P. A., & Roesch, R. (2009). *Evaluation of competence to stand trial.* New York, NY: Oxford University Press.

Zuckerman, E. L. (2005). *The clinician's thesaurus: A guidebook for wording psychological reports* (6th ed.). New York, NY: Guilford Press.

# Author Index

# Subject Index

# About the Author
# and Software Developer

**Gary Groth-Marnat, PhD,** ABPP (clinical), ABAP, is an author, lecturer, researcher, and practicing clinical psychologist and neuropsychologist. He is a fellow of the American Psychological Association (Division 12), fellow of the Society for Personality Assessment, board certified with the American Board of Professional Psychology, board certified with the American Board of Assessment Psychology, and a licensed psychologist in California. He is an Emeritus Professor at Pacifica Graduate Institute and has been a lecturer at Curtin University (Western Australia, Australia) and Deakin University (Victoria, Australia). In addition, he has been involved in clinical work through private practice and clinical consultation. Dr. Groth-Marnat is the author *Handbook of Psychological Assessment, Neuropsychological Assessment in Clinical Practice: A Guide to Test Interpretation and Integration, Integrative Assessment of Adult personality, Psychological Testing and Assessment,* and over 160 journal articles, monographs, and chapters in books.

**Ari Davis is currently a PhD** candidate in clinical psychology at Pacifica Graduate Institute, and is in private practice in Beverly Hills and the San Fernando Valley, California. Mr. Davis is a software developer who has specialized in the development of expert systems, analysis and reporting, and assessment/diagnostic software in the medical and psychological fields. His focus in clinical psychology regards the integration of Eastern thought within the depth and psychoanalytic approaches to understanding and treating psychological and health disorders. Mr. Davis' work with Dr. Gary Groth-Marnat had been dedicated to creating an expert system tutorial and psychological report authoring application that is oriented to a therapeutic approach to psychological assessment.

# About the CD-ROM

## INTRODUCTION

This appendix provides you with information on the contents of the CD that accompanies this book. For the latest information, please refer to the ReadMe file located at the root of the CD.

## SYSTEM REQUIREMENTS

Make sure that your computer meets the minimum system requirements listed in this section. If your computer doesn't match up to most of these requirements, you may have a problem using the contents of the CD.

- A computer with a processor running at 400 Mhz or faster
- At least 64 MB of total RAM installed on your computer; for best performance, we recommend at least 128 MB
- A CD-ROM drive
- Adobe Flash Player 9 or later (free download from Adobe.com)
- Adobe Reader (free download from Adobe.com)

*Note:* Many popular word-processing programs are capable of reading Microsoft Word files. However, users should be aware that a slight amount of formatting might be lost when using a program other than Microsoft Word.

### Using the CD With Windows

To access the content from the CD, follow these steps:

1. Insert the CD into your computer's CD-ROM drive. The license agreement appears (Windows 7 > Select **Start.exe** from the AutoPlay window or follow the same steps for Windows Vista).
   The interface won't launch if you have autorun disabled. In that case, click Start > Run (for Windows Vista, Start > All Programs > Accessories > Run). In the dialog box that appears, type **D:\Start. exe**. (Replace **D** with the proper letter if your CD drive uses a different letter. If you don't know the letter, see how your CD drive is listed under My Computer.) Click **OK**.
2. Read through the license agreement, and then click the Accept button if you want to use the CD. The CD interface appears. Simply select the material you want to view.

### Using the CD With a Mac

The PC-compatible software requires Parallels or a Windows emulator to be able to function in a Mac environment.

## WHAT'S ON THE CD

The following sections provide a summary of the software and other materials you'll find on the CD.

### Content

- Psychological Report Writing Assistant (PRWA), an instructional, expert system software that guides the report writer through all phases of report development.
- PRWA user manual.

## TROUBLESHOOTING

If you have difficulty installing or using any of the materials on the companion CD, try the following solutions:

- Turn off any antivirus software that you may have running. Installers sometimes mimic virus activity and can make your computer incorrectly believe that it is being infected by a virus. (Be sure to turn the antivirus software back on later.)

- Close all running programs. The more programs you're running, the less memory is available to other programs. Installers also typically update files and programs; if you keep other programs running, installation may not work properly.
- Reboot if necessary. If all else fails, rebooting your machine can often clear any conflicts in the system.

## Customer Care

If you have trouble with the CD-ROM, please call the Wiley Product Technical Support phone number at (800) 762-2974. Outside the United States, call 1 (317) 572-3994. You can also contact Wiley Product Technical Support at **http://support.wiley.com** John Wiley & Sons will provide technical support only for installation and other general quality control items. For technical support of the applications themselves, consult the program's vendor or author.

To place additional orders or to request information about other Wiley products, please call (877) 762-2974.